Bay State Road

Bay State Road

After Twenty Years

Robert Allan Hill

RESOURCE *Publications* · Eugene, Oregon

BAY STATE ROAD
After Twenty Years

Copyright © 2025 Robert Allan Hill. All rights reserved. Except for brief quotations in critical publications or reviews, no part of this book may be reproduced in any manner without prior written permission from the publisher. Write: Permissions, Wipf and Stock Publishers, 199 W. 8th Ave., Suite 3, Eugene, OR 97401.

Resource Publications
An Imprint of Wipf and Stock Publishers
199 W. 8th Ave., Suite 3
Eugene, OR 97401

www.wipfandstock.com

PAPERBACK ISBN: 979-8-3852-5211-4
HARDCOVER ISBN: 979-8-3852-5212-1
EBOOK ISBN: 979-8-3852-5213-8
VERSION NUMBER 09/09/25

Chapters 1 and 2 of this book appeared previously in *Renewal: Thought, Word, and Deed* by Robert Allan Hill (Lanham: Hamilton Books, an imprint of Bloomsbury Publishing, Inc., 2009) and are republished with permission.

Chapters 10, 11, and 17 of this book appeared previously in *Toward a Common Hope: Chautauqua Lake Sermons* by Robert Allan Hill (Eugene, OR: Wipf & Stock, 2018) and are republished with permission.

Scripture quotations unless otherwise noted are from the New Revised Standard Version, Updated Edition. Copyright © 2021 National Council of Churches of Christ in the United States of America. Used by permission. All rights reserved worldwide.

Scripture quotations marked (KJV) are from The Authorized (King James) Version. Rights in the Authorized Version in the United Kingdom are vested in the Crown. Reproduced by permission of the Crown's patentee, Cambridge University Press.

Scripture quotations marked (RSV) are from the Revised Standard Version of the Bible, copyright © 1946, 1952, and 1971 the Division of Christian Education of the National Council of the Churches of Christ in the United States of America. Used by permission. All rights reserved.

I dedicate this book to my beloved wife
Janette Lee Pennock Hill,
whose own faithful presence and ministry across
Boston University for these past twenty years have
paved the way for the preaching of the gospel.

Contents

Introduction | ix

1. The Walk of Faith | 1
2. Take, Read | 7
3. The Partnership of the Gospel | 18
4. What a Friend We Have in . . . Paul | 26
5. Two Songs of Solomon | 35
6. Merrywood | 44
7. Remembering Howard Thurman | 52
8. Snow Day | 60
9. A Rumor of Angels | 68
10. Exit or Voice? | 76
11. Sweet Chariot | 83
12. Remembering Elie Wiesel | 89
13. Hope That is Seen is Not Hope | 98
14. Hope is the Negation of Negation | 104
15. Liberal Hope | 111
16. A Sermon on the Mound | 118
17. Faith Before Daybreak | 124
18. Luminous Eye | 130
19. After Ten Years | 140
20. Baccalaureate 2023 | 147

Bibliography | 155

Introduction

When I was the age that our entering seminarians are now, I learned to preach by reading sermons. There is something particular about the experience of reading sermons on the page: it offers the gift of careful study of substance and craft alike, at one's own pace. Insight unfolds gradually in that place wherein the voice of the preacher meets the stillness of the page.

It may be that such books as this one are now treasured more by readers my age than by the younger digital generations, and that is as it should be—times change. We at Boston University's Marsh Chapel attend to all who seek the Word: through blog posts, podcasts, and now live video. Still, I believe—perhaps quaintly, perhaps rightly—that there remains a place for a printed collection, not only as a record of ministry but as a tool for learning and formation.

The twenty sermons gathered here are drawn from across the twenty years of my deanship at Marsh Chapel. During these years, Jan and I have made our home on a quiet, tree-lined stretch of Bay State Road, in view of the Charles River, a short walk from the chapel. I have walked from that apartment to the chapel and back again, week by week, season by season, year upon year. Each sermon in this volume was written, prayed over, and preached within sight of that familiar path. Thus, *Bay State Road* means to honor the daily rhythm of a life in ministry, set within a longer arc of reflection, preaching, and faithful presence.

The collection is representative, not exhaustive—glimpses of a larger ministry rather than a full record of it. Some sermons reflect on milestones, such as the first time I preached at Marsh Chapel as its dean ("The Walk of Faith"), and a message as new graduates embarked on their next chapter

INTRODUCTION

("Baccalaureate 2023"). "After Ten Years" remembers the grief in the wake of the Boston Marathon. But most were preached on "regular" Sundays, whose very ordinariness is the canvas on which the extraordinary is made visible.

I offer them now as a contribution to the celebration of the seventy-fifth anniversary of Marsh Chapel's construction. The great voices of this pulpit—Howard Thurman, Robert Hamill, Robert Neville, and others—have modeled theological preaching of the highest order: spiritual, systematic, philosophical, biblical. Sunday by Sunday, year by year, we have sought to bear witness to the gospel in a university setting, across a culture ever in change.

Yet our goal in this season is not nostalgia, but preparation. We honor the seventy-five years behind us in order to ready the chapel for the seventy-five years ahead. I steward this space as one who believes that the pulpit must speak to culture, not retreat from it. We strive to engage the pressing concerns of the day with the lasting wisdom of scripture and the tradition of faith. The historical resonance of this pulpit must meet the urgency of our present.

Welcome, then, to twenty years of preaching from the Marsh Chapel pulpit. May these words serve again, anew, afresh.

—Rev. Dr. Robert Allan Hill
Dean of Marsh Chapel
Professor of New Testament and Pastoral Theology
Chaplain to the University
Boston University

I

The Walk of Faith

Mark 6:1–13
Delivered at Boston University Marsh Chapel
July 9, 2006

Dark

FAITH IS A WALK in the dark.

As Paul Tillich said many years ago, "Faith, formally or generally defined, is the state of being grasped . . . by the ultimate in being and meaning. . . . being grasped by an ultimate concern . . . Being grasped by the Spiritual Presence and opened."[1] Faith "is the act of keeping ourselves open to the Spiritual Presence which has grasped us and opened us."[2]

Faith is a walk forward into the unknown, into the dark and open entrance to the future.

Darkness need not surprise you. There may be no darkness in God, as 1 John declares.

But there is a lot of God in darkness. There may be no darkness in divinity, but there surely is divinity in darkness. The Bible tells us so.

In its very first sentence. In its very first sentence, the Bible tells us so. Darkness was upon the face of the deep when the divine sermon spoke

---

1. Tillich, *Systematic Theology*, 3:130.
2. Tillich, *Systematic Theology*, 3:132.

creation. Darkness. "Blacker than a hundred midnights down in a cypress swamp."[3] In the beginning, there was darkness—infused with divinity.

Darkness lurks in every scriptural nook and darkness lurks in every biblical cranny. Jacob scurries to the river called Jabbok, at night. The children of Israel would neither have heeded nor have needed a great pillar of fire, across the wilderness, except that they traveled . . . at night. Yahweh gave them a cloud of smoke—his daily obscurity—and a pillar of fire—his nightly obscurity, with which to chart their course. Obscurity squared. You remember the university professor of theology and culture, Nicodemus. Nicodemus saw the light, at night. Every Holy Week encounter happens at night. Jesus prays at night. Peter betrays at night. Thomas doubts at night. Mary shouts at night. All the crucial passion scenes occur at night. And Paul? Paul and Silas, past midnight in a Roman prison, have their chains ripped off. Their guard is petrified, but they are not surprised. The night time—is the right time.

You would like faith to be simple and sunny and clear? You would prefer that faith be as plain as the nose on your face? Or, plainer still, as plain as the nose on *my* face? Really. When has that ever been so? With Jeremiah, walking, by night, in chains, to Babylon? With Samson, blinded, seeing a lifelong night? With Paul shipwrecked? With George Washington, Christmas Eve of 1776, marching in the snow at midnight, crossing the river to Trenton, with all the chips on the table? With Harriet Tubman at 2 AM, listening for bloodhounds along the Susquehanna? Or maybe with Dwight Eisenhower at 3 AM on June 6, 1944? Or with Nelson Mandela during his twenty-eight years of darkness behind bars? No. Darkness surprises no one who lives in friendship with God, least of all you who have been baptized to the cross.

The word comes at night. First at night, in the Genesis pattern, "evening and morning . . ." The true light that enlightens everyone was coming into the world. The light shines—in the darkness.

Our Scripture today was formed, *formed* in the dark catacombs of Rome, seven decades after Christmas, and four decades after Good Friday. Mark lights a candle for faith by trying—throughout the Gospel and especially in this chapter—to answer a hard question. Why did Jesus suffer? Why did Jesus die? Why did Jesus fail? Why was the Messiah rejected, dishonored, and unheeded? Mark's first answer, in verses 1–6: so it is with prophets, especially at home. His second answer, in verses 7–13: so as to

---

3. Johnson, "The Creation," 17.

teach us to go forward into the dark, fearless. One needs no bag or second tunic, just a bit of attitude, and a whistle in the dark.

Now, if we are honest, darkness is frightening. But not unexpected. Frightening, but not surprising. It is sobering to see a loved one taken off in a stretcher, down the long night hallway of uncertainty. Human life in a nuclear age is anxious life, ever-shadowed life, lived against the background of a potential nuclear winter. Who would not sleep with one eye open, come hurricane season, when the wind begins to blow, after Katrina, after the Indian Ocean tsunami? Who is not sobered by the report of a potential subway bombing? Beware, beware a cheery, cozy, quasi Christ, unfamiliar with the dark. Beware a Jesus who has not been given his night license. Beware a loud, light, boxy, bongo, easy Christ. There are plenty around today. Stephen Prothero's excellent book *American Jesus*[4] will show you the historical bestiary. Beware a trumpeted acclamation that it is already, always morning. As in: "It's morning in America . . ." It isn't. Jesus's cross is the nighttime hallmark of his loving. In fact, in sum, his heavy walking is his loving. His departure is the heart of his loving.

You know from your experience about loving and leaving. Like a mother leaving a daughter at school, or a father leaving a son at camp, or a teacher leaving a student at graduation, or a boss leaving an apprentice at retirement, or a parent, perhaps a mother or father memorialized here today, leaving this earth. As Bonhoeffer's sturdy words remind us, the leaving is the loving:

> Nothing can make up for the absence of someone whom we love, and it would be wrong to try to find a substitute; we must simply hold out and see it through. That sounds very hard at first, but at the same time it is a great consolation, for the gap, as long as it remains unfilled, preserves the bond between us. It is nonsense to say that God fills the gap; he doesn't fill it, but on the contrary, he keeps it empty and so helps us to keep alive our former communion with each other, even at the cost of pain.[5]

The darkness is frightening, *but you need not fear it*. The edgy fragments of a postmodern sensibility—every generation and identity group for itself and the devil take the hindmost—is frightening, *but you need not fear it*. The cataclysmic demise of authentic Christianity in the Northeast—lovely, large, lasting, and liberal, and increasingly gone—is frightening, *but*

---

4. Farrar, Straus & Giroux, 2003.
5. Bonhoeffer, *Letters and Papers from Prison*, 176.

you need not fear it. The emptiness of the world when your spouse dies and you think of emptying the closets is a frightening prospect indeed, worse than death itself, *but you need not fear it*. Here is why. You come from a long line of women and men who have practiced discipleship in the dark, who have earned their night licenses, as you also have done. Your people knew God . . . at night. You will, too. Miguel de Unamuno had it right: "Warmth, warmth, more warmth! for we die of cold, and not of darkness. It is not the night that kills, but the frost."[6]

We share with the early church an experience of God at night. At their best, early believers knew how to take responsible risk. At their best, they knew how to come and to go, how to enter and to leave. At their highest, they trusted their instincts. At their finest, they had the guts to start out before dawn, before the fog lifted, before daybreak. They hoped, that is, for what they did not see. Who hopes for what he sees? We hope for what we do not see.

Do we minimize the obscurity of the future, the dark night of the unforeseen? Do we repress the forebodings of the subconscious? Do we deny the complexities of power? Do we call darkness light and night day? No. No. No. No. No.

Nothing of the night is foreign to us. Nothing of darkness is foreign to us. We avoid nothing, nothing, "though this world, with devils filled, should threaten to undo us."[7] Darkness is no surprise.

Walk

We have learned to walk in the dark.

You will not want to race in the dark, like a cabbie hurtling down Commonwealth at midnight. We do not run headlong—*foolish, faithless, heartless, ruthless*. No. We do not hurl ourselves like fools into the black beyond. You know the value of virtue: prudence, temperance, courage, patience.

Walk.

Walk humbly. If we walk, we have fellowship. Walk by faith, not sight. Walk with God. At night, especially, walk. Do not run. Walk.

Slow and steady wins the day. A stitch in time saves nine. An ounce of prevention is worth a pound of cure. Let your head save your heels. Look before you leap.

---

6. Unamuno, *Tragic Sense of Life*, 327.
7. Luther, "Majesty and Power," no. 67, st. 3.

Thunders Isaiah, "Those who wait for the Lord shall renew their strength; they shall mount up with wings like eagles; they shall run and not be weary; they shall walk and not faint."[8] Those today sensing a call to the ministry want to remember Isaiah.

Ghandi weighed a hundred pounds, wore a sari, and looked sorrier. He walked four miles a day. And, oh, by the way—he changed the world for the better. Jesus never left Palestine. He walked, preaching and teaching and healing. John Wesley walked slowly to Aldersgate Street, and more slowly home, a changed man. His horse walked all over England. Morality, generosity, piety followed the man on horseback. Said Wesley, "I am always in haste, but never in a hurry."[9] James Bashford peers down upon us from the stained glass of this hallowed space. He took his time: First as pastor (his highest honor), then as president of Ohio Wesleyan, then as the first Methodist bishop in China. His way of living, of walking, inspired a generation to take the world and make it young again. Like Branch Rickey, who integrated baseball. (*But that was last week's sermon!*) Easy, slow. Walk. Saunter. Lollygag.

Self-destruction awaits a hasty pace in the dark. On the downside, Methodists and others have sometimes been hasty about doing all the good we can. Sometimes we are too optimistic in our accounting. We accentuate the positive, which is alright, but suffocate the negative, which is not alright. We engage in wishful thinking, sometimes, when it comes to money. We see what we want to see, rather than what is. After all, were we not meant to be "happy in God"? The newspapers this week, or a great history like David Hempton's *Methodism: Empire of the Spirit*,[10] or our own experience itself, will confirm our penchant for hasty counting, and even for tragically overoptimistic accounting.

Take your time at night. Feel your way. Step along. Be careful. Once the toothpaste is out of the tube, it is very hard to get it back in. Let your eyesight grow accustomed to the obscurity of experience and the hidden nature of God. Befriend shadows. Walk. Skulk. Lurk. Who hopes for what he sees?

Abraham Heschel would call this Sabbath living: "There is a realm of time where the goal is not to have but to be, not to own but to give, not to control but to share, not to subdue but to be in accord. . . . The higher

---

8. Isa 40:31, NRSVUE.
9. Wesley, *Works*, 12:287.
10. Yale University Press, 2005.

goal of spiritual living is not to amass a wealth of information, but to face sacred moments."[11]

To face sacred moments.

Walk. Swing your arms. Smile. Greet your neighbors and their wayward kids. Take your time. Only the devil has no time to let things grow. It is a foolish farmer who pulls up his carrots every week to check their progress. Easy, easy.

Otherwise, you will miss the fullness of life and faith.

Dietrich Bonhoeffer, born one hundred years ago this year, a great interpreter in word and life of Mark 6, is best remembered for his teaching, by word and sacrifice, about grace, and his reverence for the walk of faith announced in today's Gospel.

> Cheap grace is the preaching of forgiveness without requiring repentance, baptism without church discipline, Communion without confession, absolution without personal confession. Cheap grace is grace without discipleship, grace without the cross, grace without Jesus Christ, living and incarnate. . . .
>
> Costly grace is the gospel which must be *sought* again and again, the gift which must be *asked* for, the door at which a man must *knock*.
>
> Such grace is *costly* because it calls us to follow, and it is *grace* because it calls us to follow *Jesus Christ*. It is costly because it costs a man his life, and it is grace because it gives a man the only true life.[12]

Costly grace takes time. It requires us to walk, and not faint. Costly grace takes time. Time to invite, and to tithe. Time to fish and to plant. Faith begins with giving away 10 percent of what we earn, and ends in inviting someone to dinner.

The only way to make headway in the dark is to walk. The night time is the right time—if you will walk.

Victor Hugo wrote: "Courage, then, and patience! Courage for the great sorrows of life, and patience for the small ones. And then when you have laboriously accomplished your daily task, go to sleep in peace. God is awake."[13]

Here is the good news: Faith . . . is . . . a walk . . . in the dark.

---

11. Heschel, *Sabbath*, 4, 6.
12. Bonhoeffer, *Cost of Discipleship*, 44-45. (Italics in the original.)
13. Hugo, *Letters*, 23.

2

Take, Read

Matthew 9:9–13
Delivered at Boston University School of Theology
Matriculation 2006

Preface

MANY OF US ARE quite new here. We hardly know each others' names, let alone see each others' hearts. We learn one name at a time, I and thou.

At Chautauqua in 1999, I introduced myself to a frail saint who asked my name, heard it, and chuckled. Hill is not a colorful enough surname to become much of a source of hilarity, but she chuckled still. She explained. "You know, I had such a fear of asking people their names again, once they had told me, that I came up with a system that invariably worked. Rather than saying, 'I have forgotten your name, please remind me,' or something equally honest, I would say, 'Now, tell me again, do you spell your last name with an *i* or an *e*?' My technique succeeded." Chuckle. "Until I used it with a man who shares your surname. 'Do you spell your last name with an *i* or an *e*?' He blustered. 'My name is Hill, not Hell, you spell it *H I L L*!' "

Caught between our own identities, and visions for the future both heavenly and hellish, we have arrived in Boston. Like Matthew, who in chapter 9 paints himself, as Velázquez did, into his own portrait, we are invited. *Follow me.* "He comes to us as One unknown, without a name, as of old . . . He speaks to us the same word: 'Follow thou me!'"[1] wrote Schweitzer. The real moment of real invitation and real response is real apocalypse. Paul said he met Jesus "by apocalypse." I am here by apocalypse. Another story for another day. You may be, too. What are we doing here?

We are here for matriculation, to begin, to exchange one maternity for another. Here is a matriculation account. Vernon Jordan went to Depauw (a small Methodist school for small Methodists, led by various BU graduates), in Indiana. From their home in Louisiana, his dad, mom, and younger siblings drove him up—"up south," as Dr. King might have said—and dropped him off there in Greencastle. Weeping, his father evidently said, "Vernon, we are not coming back until four years from now. You are here where your future opens. We will be here at your graduation, sitting in the front row. This is your time. I have one word of advice: Read. When others are playing, you read. When others are sleeping, you read. When others are drinking, you read. When others are partying, you read." Take, Vernon, take and read.

In mid-September of 1976, perhaps thirty years ago to the very day, many of us stood in the common room at the Union Theological Seminary. I stood near Linda Clarke and Horace Allen, and among the ghosts of theologians past that haunted those halls as others of equal tremor do these. George Landes spoke for the biblical field. Sanders, Terrien, Brown, and Martyn sat behind him. "There has been some question about whether the Bible is relevant," Landes said quietly, this exacting teacher of Hebrew, and noted Jonah scholar. "We in the biblical field"—here he gestured meaningfully to his esteemed colleagues—"ask that before you settle that question, whether or not the Bible is relevant, that you . . . read it." That is what I remember, in sum, from the days of entry into theological study. Those days themselves were not easy, but I cannot tell you, in retrospect, just how majestically meaningful the voices in that room, many now dead, have been to me. They are in my ears. They are here beside me. Just as the theological voices of this uniquely exciting, young, potent new faculty of the Boston University School of Theology will be for many, for many years to come. May your retrospective in 2036 be similar. I hope you, three decades hence, will remember something similar. Whatever others do in these precious days of somehow-subsidized freedom, *you read*. Read. The savings habits of careful reading can become the difference between life and death.

---

1. Schweitzer, *Quest of the Historical Jesus*, 401.

Matthew on Taking and Reading

Matthew says go and learn, follow and discern, take and read. Matthew, the author of a dark Gospel, reflecting, perhaps, the persecutions of the late first century, has stitched together his own matriculation to faith with an apothegm (that is a word that you never use in a sermon) about reading. His entry involved reading. "Go and learn." Why should anyone have needed to learn the meaning of such a fine and famous line from Hosea, about mercy and sacrifice? Evidently, the meaning was far from evident by the time of Matthew's suffering. More study was needed. Why? The experience of the fragile church of the late first century required new readings of the inherited traditions of the church. Here is the preacher's task, to translate tradition into insights for effective living.

Each Synoptic passage is like a choral piece, including four voices. There is the soprano voice of Jesus of Nazareth, embedded somewhere in the full harmonic mix. In Matthew 9, Jesus conflicts with the Pharisaic aversion to pagan inscriptions and iconography. There is the alto voice of the primitive church, arguably always the most important of the four voices, that which carries the forming of the passage in the needs of the community. From Mark to Matthew an insertion has arisen, the citation of Hosea 6:6. Evidently, as the earliest church moved farther out and away from the memory of Jesus, it needed the fuller support of the prophetic tradition—mercy, not sacrifice, compassion, not holiness. The tenor line is that of the evangelist. Matthew is here, marking his own appearance in the record. His work seems to reflect a connection to school, to scribes—perhaps, as Stendahl said years ago from across the river, to Qumrān. The baritone is borne by later interpretation, to begin soon with Irenaeus, "Against Heresies": "What doctor, when wishing to cure a sick man, would act in accordance with the desires of the patient, and not in accordance with the requirements of medicine?"[2] If our church music carries only one line, we may be tempted to interpret our Scripture with only one voice, and miss the SATB harmonies therein, to our detriment.

There are two steps in today's Gospel: Take, read. The first is invitation, offered and received. The second is education, prepared and planned. You have, somehow, washed up on this shore, out of the ranges of materialism all around. You have set aside more lucrative degrees, you have refrained from taking more reliable paths, and you have stepped aside from entering

---

2. Irenaeus, "Against Heresies," 1:377.

upon more pleasant routines. What were you thinking? You are here thanks to somebody, and some potent word of invitation. Then, too, you are here to learn. To learn what the ancient world still thought was obscure, even following Hosea and Plato: God delights in mercy. I desire (in Greek, *thelo*), I delight in, enjoy, am happy for, celebrate, am passionate about . . . mercy.

One wonders just how pointed is Matthew's reference here in regard to his own community. Is the contrast between the partnership of the gospel and the willingness to suffer in the coliseum? Or the choice between a hearty entrance into some of the culture around, rather than a sacrificial abstemiousness about the world? Or the happy delight in new deliverance, over against the trudging discipline of mature faith? What of mercy, and what of sacrifice? What pastoral visit and what new learning has formed this passage? Go . . . and learn. Take . . . and read.

Point One: Take

Close reading is crucial to health.

One day, following the morning service, we visited a dear saint in her home. She had been in hospital that week, and sat recuperating in her parlor. Her family was with her. And she had a story to tell.

That Tuesday, she prepared to be taken by ambulance from one hospital to another, for a particular procedure. She is a fine, older Methodist lady, so she prepared herself with what dignity one can muster in a hospital bed, robed in a hospital gown and alone in the corridor of life. A little makeup, a comb and brush, some careful adjustments of remaining raiment, glasses perched, smile shining.

She could see the elevator door open, and her stretcher moving out. The attendants clearly mentioned her name as they signed the paperwork at the desk. The nurse motioned across the hall in the general direction of her room. She poised herself, prepared to be a good, courteous patient. Down the hall the men came, and she waved. They returned the gesture. To her door they rolled—and then, remarkably, rolled on by! They passed to the next room—129, not 128, such a small difference—a room inhabited alone by a kindly woman who is deaf as a post. "Mrs. Smith?" "Yes," she replied, her volume in inverse proportion to her accuracy. Into the stretcher went the wrong woman, and down the hall they moved. My dear parishioner called out, used her buzzer, flailed her arms like a dancer around a campfire. But in a New York minute they were gone, carrying away the wrong person. On the way home, following the procedure, someone apparently had the presence of mind to look at the stretchered woman's wrist band, her name tag. I wonder how the reader felt not to see the name Smith. A rare moment of revelation. In this case, little lasting harm occurred. Our hospitals, in fact, to my eye, given their hourly commitment to excellence and attention to detail, put other institutions to shame. We all know the fear of the wrong arm amputated, the wrong knee replaced, the wrong woman put in the stretcher. Physician's malpractice. But the news, good news, of medical malpractice is that you know soon—an hour, a day, a decade—what has happened, and you can endure it or correct it. So it goes with the physician's malpractice.

Not so with the metaphysician's.

Biological error lasts, at most, a lifetime. Theological error resides for three generations, or more. If, as Martin Luther King Sr. supposedly said, "it takes three generations to make a preacher," then it also takes three generations, or more, to recognize and correct the effects of metaphysical malpractice. You cannot fully see its effect for twenty or forty or sixty or eighty years. And it is a short way from birdie to bogie, from clean cuts to nicks and scratches in innocent organs, mistaken severations and amputations, blood spilled and shed in the wrong bed. Choose the physical mistakes, for the metaphysical are so much more insidious, more damaging, more real. Read carefully the signs of the times, and their distinctive differences.

There is a crucial difference between sacrifice and mercy. There is a crucial difference between holiness and compassion. There is a crucial difference between law and love. There is a crucial difference between representation and redemption. There is a crucial difference between incantation and incarnation. There is a crucial difference between innocence and integrity. There is a crucial difference between independence and interdependence. There is a crucial difference between Christology and theology. There is a crucial difference between giving and tithing.

When we let the very worthy interests in representation eclipse the main work of the gospel, in redemption, we are making a surgical mistake.

We risk harm when we replace incarnation with incantation, forgetting that the Sabbath was made for humankind, not humankind for the Sabbath.

Integrity and holiness survive beyond innocence, so we might say: In singleness integrity; in partnership fidelity.

We risk harm when we replace "just war" with just "war," interdependence with independence. The 2003 invasion of Iraq jettisoned our inherited experience codified in just war theory. It was preemptive, unilateral, imperial, unforeseeable, not responsive, multilateral, restorative, and limited.

We are still wallowing, as Doug Hall warned a generation ago (you see, it does take a long time), in a Unitarianism of the Second Person of the Trinity.

There is a world of difference between habit and mercy, contribution and generosity, giving and tithing. The pervasive materialism of our culture receives its rejection in tithing, not in mere giving. The enduring sense of entitlement in our county receives its contradiction in tithing, not in mere giving. The abject loneliness of exurban life receives its denial in tithing, not in mere giving

These are crucial distinctions. How are we ever going to make them, and learn to make them consistently, to avoid metaphysical misdirection?

Point Two: Read

How are we to take up the stressful work, the hard labor of careful practice?

We go and read.

Find yourself on a bench in front of the sculpture of Arthur Fiedler. Sit along the river as the sun sets. Make permanent friends with the quiet pews of Marsh Chapel and the hidden crannies of the library. Locate that 2 AM diner breakfast that helped Fred Craddock become a preacher. Find the Arthur Fiedler reading room, a beautiful spot. When others are at war with administration, you read. When others are cursing their bishops, you read. When others are finding fault with faculty hairstyles, you read. You may especially want to read those who have lived through other times of ruin. Reading frees you from the twenty-first century. Reading cuts you loose from your own time and place. Others, too, have taught and preached in the ruins of the church.

I picture a bright autumn day. You are walking the emerald necklace, with lunch and a bag full of books.

You start out at Charlesgate, thinking about reading today....

You live in a country in which 40 percent of the population can name each of The Three Stooges, and fewer than 5 percent can name the Ten Commandments. Literacy has a new meaning, referring not to those who can read, but to those who do read. We are preparing for teaching and ministry among those who do read, or will soon.

You think of a little office in the World Council of Churches. In that office sat Paolo Freire, brown bag lunch in hand, who taught a continent, for its liberation, to read . . .

You remember the line, from *A River Runs Through It*,[3] that Methodists are Baptists who can read. But today, the literate are not those who can, but those who do read.

Close, careful reading matters. I believe Colin Powell could testify to the difference between close, exacting reading, and visual learning. But he is only a mirror upon ourselves. What have we been reading, as a people? Not enough world history. Not enough comparative religion. Not enough detailed daily news. Not enough economics or political science. Certainly not enough of the *koine* Greek of Matthew 9, or the Hebrew verbs of Hosea 6.

You pause to sit at the Fenway gardens to read books from the BU School of Theology, past and future . . .

The future of the globe relies not on those who can read, but on those who do. Allan Knight Chalmers, here in the 1950s, taught his students to read a book a day.

Elmer Leslie, around the same time, wrote, interpreting Psalm 1. His book *The Psalms* concluded with Psalm 1.

> The psalmist first describes negatively the man who walks life's good way, that is, by what he does not do. He refuses to walk as the morally loose, criminal element in society counsel him to do, or to stand where those congregate who have missed life's true goal, or to sit as a willing crony among those who scoff at goodness. Then the psalmist turns to positive description and depicts a good man in terms of what he does. He delights in religion and meditates upon the Lord's requirements as enjoined in the law, brooding over them by day and in the wakeful hours of the night.[4]

From one corner, learn with A. T. Pierson to "sanctify ambition rather than to crucify it."[5] A close distinction in a careful reading of life. From another corner, learn the nature of "Good Samaritan" Christians. From another, learn with nineteenth-century Methodism the lasting danger of

---

3. "The Burns family . . . were Methodists, who my father called 'Baptists who could read.'" Redford, dir., *A River Runs Through It*.

4. Leslie, *Psalms*, 432.

5. Pierson, *Arthur T. Pierson*, 59.

poor financial planning, and learn the merits of disciplined sacramental observance. Or, learn the history of 3 Timothy. All this and more, you can read in the books of your teachers in this fine school. Read what you want, what you need, when you want, as you need.

You sit beside the lawn at Emmanuel College, to pray . . .

In our own reforming, newly reconstituted community here at the BU School of Theology, we have been further chastened and strongly sobered by death coming as a thief in the night. In one sense, there is little we can say, either to others or to ourselves. We must hold our tongue, and stand, and, just like a preacher, wait and wring our hands. We do not know why these things happen. There is no explaining, finally, the depth of tragic loss. But we can be present to one another, and treat each other with an honest kindness, a kind honesty. And with a little humility about our own limitations. And with a happy grace that embraces every morning with a sense of wonder. G. K. Chesterton taught it right, as he did so often: "The world does not lack for wonders, only for a sense of wonder."[6] This harrowing week does not lack for meanings, but only for a sense of meaning. We can trust the unseen God to give confidence, faith, and your lived capacity to withstand what you cannot understand. Sometimes that is all you have—the faith to withstand what you cannot understand. For the loss of a brother does not make this week, this matriculation, any less meaningful, or less meaning filled. In fact, it frames our study in the arch of eternity, and recalls for us the heart of ministry, which is the health of persons, the saving of souls. We are on the edge of eternity in every moment of life. You, teacher, you preacher, you pastor, are living testimony to the Eternal Now.

You pause and rest at the beginning of the Riverway to think practically about theological education . . .

The ministry will be upon you in three years, or less, or more. If, by reading, you can start to think theologically, and model that dimension of spirituality for your parishioners, you will have done them a world of good.

Students, read the bottom line. You need to leave seminary with no debt. Faculty, read for the fine truth that sets free. Teachers, love your subjects and your students, as Augustine advised. You have nothing to do but to know the truth. Administration, read the need for joyful conviviality. Minimize debt, students. Marginalize delusion, faculty. Maximize community, administration.

---

6. Coffin, *Collected Sermons*, 1:293.

Oh, I know there is more to life than books. I remember the 1904 *Discipline* and its terse rebuke that "we ought to throw by all the libraries in the world, rather than be guilty of the loss of one soul."[7] The difference, a hundred years later, is that for the soul of the world not to perish, you must become living libraries. Bradbury's campfire at the end of *Fahrenheit 451* comes to mind.

You find a quiet corner along the river to think about the impact of careful reading, and its absence . . .

This fall we shall witness a titanic struggle for the minds and hearts of America. We do not cast a single ballot in any direction. But the difference between a fear-soaked visual bombardment and a careful literate philosophy of peace is close to the marrow of what will, or will not, save us. What some discern as the shift from a gender divide to a religious divide should perhaps be seen as a literacy divide. It matters what hymns, prayers, liturgy, and certainly sermons people know.

One does not live by bread alone. Better read than dead. "Better well hung than ill wed,"[8] better well-read than spiritually dead.

Read now. Robert F. Kennedy did not have the freedom to do a research paper on Aeschylus the night Martin Luther King Jr. was killed. He either had read or he hadn't. He had. His three minutes in the Indianapolis rain were his greatest words, because he had read.

There is very little left of the historic Protestant church in the Northeast. What there is clings for life to the words, and to the Word.

In the glade, you wonder about the nature of reading itself . . .

And what relationship shall the reader have to the read? Who among us does anywhere near enough to deconstruct our own various contexts? Is the text to have the sole divining voice, or is the reader king? What of the relationship between the unsaid and the uttered? In reading, how do ranges of power dance with colors of truth? Is the truth of Scripture the sole truth?

---

7. Andrews, ed., *Doctrines and Discipline*, 141.

8. Søren Kierkegaard's motto "Better well hung than ill wed" appears in his book *Philosophical Fragments*. Commentary by Niels Thulstrup explains that "Kierkegaard took his motto from Shakespeare's *Twelfth Night*, Act I, Scene V (clown speaking to Maria): 'Many a good hanging prevents a bad marriage.' . . . The meaning of the motto is explained in the preface to *Concluding Unscientific Postscript* (p. 3) : 'Undisturbed, and in compliance with his own motto: "Better well hung than ill wed," the well-hung [crucified with Christ] author has been left hanging. . . . Better so, better well hung than by an unfortunate marriage brought into systematic relationship with all the world.' " Kierkegaard, *Philosophical Fragments*, 152.

Or one truth among many? Or *primus inter pares*? Or an anachronism altogether? How, then, do you read?

Misreading intelligence can land a nation in the soup of a civil war. Misreading tests can land a patient in the wrong surgical suite. Misreading accounts payable can land a business in bankruptcy. Misreading a traffic signal can land you in the ditch. Most of these have healing solutions available within one generation. Theological misreading lasts for several generations. It takes three or four generations to bring correction to a sincere or not so authentic theological misreading. Be careful how you read, for how you read is how you think, and how you think is how you act.

You may circle the pond at Jamaica Plains, eat lunch, and read especially from those who have read and preached in various conditions of the ruins of the church . . .

Here is an October Saturday in the sun. Read in the ruins. Take, read. Read along with those who also rose to preaching amid the ruins of the church. You walk. You read B. B. Taylor, *Leaving Church*. You walk. You read K. Phillips, *American Theocracy*. You walk. At Jamaica Pond you read P. Beinart, *The Good Fight*. Then you read Václev Havel, on almost anything. You read H. Thurman, *Jesus and the Disinherited*. Boston is your campus.

McCourt in *Angela's Ashes* is really giving you a hymn to language. He sits by the hospital bed of his eleven-year-old girlfriend. She teaches him a poem, "The Highwayman," and she dies. He is so hungry that he finds a soiled newspaper in which the daily fish and chips have been wrapped, and licks the grease . . . and the words . . . off the paper. That is, McCourt's lovely *bildungsroman* ends with the young boy escaping his past, escaping his family of origin, escaping the biology that threatens always to become full destiny, and feeding himself. He is so hungry that he finds trashed newspapers with the remains of fish and chips, and he licks the papers clean of scraps and bits and crumbs and oil, until the words on the paper fill his mouth. His whole book is about his deliverance, how he learned to live by reading, how he learned to love through words.

At last, as night is falling, you pause for a minute on the way home to read this last passage from Augustine's Confessions . . .

> I was saying these things and weeping in the most bitter contrition of my heart, when suddenly I heard the voice of a boy or a girl—I know not which—coming from the neighboring house, chanting over and over again, "Pick it up, read it; pick it up, read it [*Tolle lege, tolle lege*]." Immediately I ceased weeping and began most

earnestly to think whether it was usual for children in some kind of game to sing such a song, but I could not remember ever having heard the like. So, damming the torrent of my tears, I got to my feet, for I could not but think that this was a divine command to open the Bible and read the first passage I should light upon. For I had heard how Anthony, accidentally coming into church while the gospel was being read, received the admonition as if what was read had been addressed to him: "Go and sell what you have and give it to the poor, and you shall have treasure in heaven; and come and follow me." By such an oracle he was forthwith converted to thee.

So I quickly returned to the bench where Alypius was sitting, for there I had put down the apostle's book when I had left there. I snatched it up, opened it, and in silence read the paragraph on which my eyes first fell: "Not in rioting and drunkenness, not in chambering and wantonness, not in strife and envying, but put on the Lord Jesus Christ, and make no provision for the flesh to fulfill the lusts thereof." I wanted to read no further, nor did I need to. For instantly, as the sentence ended, there was infused in my heart something like the light of full certainty and all the gloom of doubt vanished away.[9]

At dinner, someone may ask what the matriculation sermon on Wednesday was about. You would say: "Well, I think he was singing a song of love for reading; I think he was raising a hymn of praise for reading; I think he was lining out a psalm of affirmation for reading."

Tolle, lege.

---

9. Augustine, *Confessions*, 145-46.

3

The Partnership of the Gospel

Luke 13:31–35
Delivered at Boston University Marsh Chapel
Service of Installation: March 4, 2007

Welcome

WE HAVE BEEN GATHERED here, from Texas and Chicago, from Rochester and Providence, from Bay State Road and Brookline, gathered by grace. From a university president to a babe in the womb, from the least to the greatest, we are, for a moment, gathered. As Thornton Wilder wrote, "Just for a moment now we're all together. . . . *Let's look at one another.*"[1] Let us meet the moment, not miss it. Like a mother hen gathers her brood, the Spirit of Christ has gathered us and welcomed us again into real life, which is *the partnership of the Gospel*. Welcome, and please know how meaningful your own presence truly is for this gathering.

A sermon like this one, a salutation, ought to begin with some recognition of the difficulty involved in interpretation, and perhaps with a bit of humor. To those twin ends, we recall the account of the man who was stopped for driving ninety miles an hour on the turnpike. He explained his velocity to the officer by saying he had seen a sign that said "90," so

---

1. Wilder, *Our Town*, 99. (Italics in the original.)

he drove 90. Then the officer noticed three petrified and terrified backseat riders, and asked if they were frightened by their turnpike ride. One said, "Oh no, Route 90 was fine, we just hope and pray he is not going back onto Route 220—that was really scary!" Interpretation is a delicate art. A gospel text needs and deserves some exegetical examination, and some theological explanation, and some practical application.

Exegetical Examination

In fact, our lesson today, Luke 13:31 to 35, exudes as poignant, as heartfelt, as realistic, and as personal an outlook as one can find anywhere in the Gospels, in its soprano voice of the lingering teaching of Jesus, or in its alto voice of the earliest church's memory, or in its tenor voice of the Gospel author, or in its baritone rendering in tradition.

The highest note is Jesus's own. Jesus's melody is a kind of dominical soprano voice, laden with maternal imagery today. *As a hen gathers her brood, would I have gathered you.*[2] Lines 31 to 33 are found only in Luke, and clearly go back to Jesus himself. The nature imagery, the kindliness of the Pharisees, the use of the term "fox" (from a country preacher's lexicon), the gritty undercurrent of fear, the poetry of three days: *mirable dictum!* we hear today what Jesus said. His voice, in these verses, carries across two millennia. "Go and tell that fox . . . today and tomorrow, and on the third day . . . As a hen gathers her brood . . ." Here is Jesus of Nazareth, in AD 33, facing the tragic sense of life.

(There also is his frightened, hopeful church, in AD 70, facing the tragic sense of life. There is Luke, in AD 90, facing the tragic sense of life. And here we are, gathered as partners in the Gospel. Thoreau wrote: "If it is not a tragical life we live, then I know not what to call it. Such a story as that of Jesus Christ—the history of Jerusalem, say, being a part of the Universal History. The naked, the embalmed, unburied death of Jerusalem amid its desolate hills—think of it."[3])

Listen particularly, just for moment, to the voice of the writer, Luke—the third, or tenor line, if you will, in this harmonic composition. Luke makes two novel moves that differ from the interpretation offered by Matthew, with whom Luke shares a use of a portion of this text. Both moves impress us today.

2. See: Luke 13:34, NRSVUE.
3. Thoreau, *Writings*, 1:67.

First, Luke uses two powerful, forceful verbs to show the sweep of Jesus's divine embrace, the gathering motion of the mother hen, the announcement of partnership, divine and human (*thelo* and *sunago*).[4] *I would have done . . . I would have done . . . I longed, desired, deeply wished . . . to gather, to embrace, to join together, to partner . . .* There is a deeply moving aspect to this emphasis, as Luke has Jesus open the next several chapters of the Gospel of Luke, which include all the favorite and solely Lukan materials. We have the Good Samaritan, thanks to Luke. And the lost sheep and coin, thanks to him. We have the prodigal son, that most gnostic of parables, thanks to Luke. And the dishonest steward, thanks to him. *Luke is probing the partnership of the Gospel,* and he begins his own emphasis right here. *What we think about God determines how we live. Luke illumines that partnership.*

Second, Luke stands Matthew's interpretation of expectation on its head. For Matthew, the prediction of the coming of the Son of Man was an "end of the world" prediction. Not for Luke. Matthew looks up; Luke looks out. Luke sees the world a little more as we do, with miles to go before we sleep, with generations to go before we sleep. We have work to do. Here. Now. In partnership. Together. In real unity, not just in passing togetherness. Where Matthew heralds *parousia*, Luke heralds incarnation, and the coming entry, triumphal entry, into Jerusalem. Here Luke foreshadows what is to come. According to Luke, and as George Buttrick might have said, Jesus was killed by the insurrectionists in the mob and by the reactionaries in the temple[5] (a good warning about the far left as well as the right). We can, in our time, learn from this text, and offer a form for its theological explanation.

Theological Explanation

Gathered here are we, in Boston, the cradle of liberty, and at Boston University, the cradle of Methodist ministry. It is hard to walk much farther east, without some swimming trunks. It is hard to walk much farther back, without some memories. John Adams and John Dempster would like a word or two with us. The church whose educational project Dempster, a Mohawk valley native, began, here, and the country whose cultural project

---

4. From Greek: *thelo*, to want, to wish, to will, to intend; *sunago*, to gather together, to collect, to assemble.

5. See, for example: Charles N. Davidson Jr., "George Arthur Buttrick: Christocentric Preacher and Pacifist," *Journal of Presbyterian History* (1962-1985), Vol. 53, No. 2 (Summer 1975), 143-167.

Adams, a Braintree native, began, here, both depend on human freedom, human grace.

I longed... to gather... God in Christ invites a partnership of the Gospel, as Paul names it in Philippians 1: a partnership, a *koinonia*, a partnership. (Tragically, the NRSV has rendered the word, there, a "sharing."[6] How pale, how "us," today.) *Sursum Corda*: Jesus gathers us to live out a muscular partnership of the Gospel: to learn not only to chew, but also to choose.

Our lesson shows Jesus, fully human as well as a body of divinity, the transcript in time of who God is in eternity.

T.[7] Here Jesus loves his own people like a momma, like a mother hen. These people, and we too, we could discern then, must not have been totally depraved.

U. Here Jesus recognizes the choices that inevitably make us who we are. Choice is relational and conditional, and makes us inspect what condition our condition is in. These people, and we too, must have not been unconditionally elected.

L. Here Jesus gathers everybody, all, all, like a hen with a brood. These people, and we too, we could discern then, must not have been limited to the very narrow, tiny minority of the predestined elect.

I. Here Jesus faces, heartsick, the brutal truth: that these people, and we ourselves, can and do resist the invitations of love, even the momma-like, mother love of a hen gathering chicks. They must not have been powerless. Jesus's grace was resisted, steadily and effectively, to the path of the cross.

P. Here Jesus himself does not persevere, not at least in Jerusalem, or in the spiritual culture of our time, nor does his cause, at least not in this passage. Persecution, not perseverance, awaits this holy one.

Jesus, here, means freedom. The one requirement of your picture of God is that God must be "worshippable," worthy of worship (neither cruel, nor evil, nor blind, nor capricious, nor us on our worst day). Today Jesus sets us on a path of freedom—a good Boston theme. Human freedom that

---

6. The updated edition of the NRSV (NRSVUE) translates *koinonia* as "partnership." "I thank my God for every remembrance of you, always in every one of my prayers for all of you, praying with joy for your partnership in the gospel from the first day until now." Phil 1:3-5, NRSVUE.

7. TULIP is a theological acronym developed by John Calvin (1509-64) to summarize God's sovereignty in salvation. The five letters of the acronym stand for: total depravity, unconditional election, limited atonement, irresistible grace, and perseverance of the saints. See, for example: David N. Steele and Curtis C. Thomas, *The Five Points of Calvinism: Defined, Defended, Documented* (Phillipsburg, NJ: Presbyterian & Reformed Publishing, 1984).

is *temporal, universal, loving, imaginative, and powerful*. We will think of it in a moment as another kind of TULIP formula. We hunger for the partnership of the Gospel, the partnership of grace, divine and human, and the partnership of freedom, divine and human.

A sermon like this one, a salutation, ought to continue with some analysis and examination, careful examination, and perhaps a touch of humor. To those twin ends, Mark Trotter reminded me once of the physician who provided a thorough medical exam to one patient, declaring him as "healthy as a horse." As the man took up his coat to go, he fell down dead as a doornail. The secretary overheard the thud, entered, and asked, "What are we to do?" To which the doctor, in view of misdiagnosis, said, "Well, I don't know. But at least could we turn him around so that it looks like he's coming in, not going out?" Be wary of overly optimistic charts, graphs, reports, diagnoses. Keep the verses of Yeats at hand: "The center cannot hold . . ."[8]

For all our warlike failings, there is still a grandeur to the human being, a grandeur personally known in love, and that love modeled after its partner in the divine love—"love divine, all loves excelling"![9] (But not erasing!)

The personalist liberals of Boston knew about partnership—Brightman and his dark God-Given,[10] Ferré and his hymn to love,[11] and our own colleagues on imagination and creation. Yet they underestimated the power of human freedom for evil. Their editors and the midcourse correctors of the neoorthodox school knew about partnership. Yet they underestimated the power of human freedom for good. Their successors, the liberationists, knew about human freedom. Yet they underestimated the power of human freedom to reach across inherited boundaries.

Many decades ahead of his time, one voice stood out, and from this very pulpit. Howard Thurman explicitly championed the partnership of the Gospel. Oh, he celebrated personality with his teachers, but knew the darker dimensions of experience for both Jesus and the disinherited.[12] Oh,

---

8. Yeats, "The Second Coming," 19.

9. Wesley, "Love Divine, All Loves Excelling," no. 372, st. 1.

10. Edgar Sheffield Brightman's concept of "The Given" related to ideas about the finiteness of God. See, for example: Brightman, *The Problem of God* (1930) and *A Philosophy of Religion* (1940).

11. The work of Nels F. S. Ferré was strongly influenced by *agape* (from Greek, "selfless love") theology. See, for example: Ferré, *Swedish Contributions to Modern Theology* (1939), *Christianity and Society* (1950), and *The Christian Understanding of God* (1951).

12. A reference to Thurman, *Jesus and the Disinherited* (New York: Abingdon-Cokesbury, 1949).

he too acclaimed faith, but knew the dangers of Christo-monism, and the neglect of a common ground. Oh, he too faced the terrors of power without truth, but knew the dangers of any ghetto, and could preach a scandalous universality, and acclaim a spiritual presence. Brightman and Niebuhr and Gutiérrez all offer something, but not enough, not alone. Not enough for a world hungry for the partnership of the Gospel. Thurman would have gathered them together, like a mother hen gathering her chicks.

How shall we appropriate such an explanation? As my grandmother would admonish, "give us something practical to take home."

Practical Application

Jan and I have come to Boston to spend the fourth part of our ministry in gathering chicks, in a generative mode *and in a spirit of partnership*—to build a congregation, and recruit preachers, and exemplify spiritual hospitality, in a way that engages the next generation in the partnership of the Gospel. A national voice, a Methodist ethos, an excellent hospitality—these are our signposts. Marsh Chapel can become *a heart for the heart of the city and a worship service for the service of the city*. We will, rightly, be measured by the kind of people we produce and the kind of pastors we produce. Humanly speaking, the death or life of the church depends on the leadership of the church, and its voice. The voice of responsible Christian liberalism may be dormant but is not dead, not yet. You are here today because you are the natural partners in this expression of the Gospel. Our voice is a responsible Christian liberal voice, one that sails between the Scylla of reaction and the Charybdis of rejection. The voice of Marsh Chapel is a responsibly Christian liberalism.

A real partnership of the Gospel will depend on a common hope. It is not enough for us to recall the common faith of John Dewey. It is not enough for us to recall the common ground of Howard Thurman. On a reliable, common hope hangs our future. What are the features of the common hope, this partnership, this partnership of the Gospel? We have preached some of them this year. *T*: something temporal; a heart for the heart of the city—a longing to heal the spiritual culture of the land. *U*: something universal; an interreligious setting. *L*: something of love; a developed expression of contrition. *I*: something imaginative; a keen sense of imagination. *P*: some real power; an openness to power and presence. Today, come

Installation Sunday, a capacity for partnership, heart to heart, that rests on a faith in the partnership of God in the Gospel.

The human being, for all his and her faults, has a capacity for wonder, for love, for courage, for the mutuality of work in partnership, on which this fragile globe depends. As Charles Darwin's exhibit reminds us, for all the changes that reason and experience have brought us—which we need not fear—"there is a grandeur in this view of life . . ."[13] Nearby we have leading thinkers who write about imagination with creativity and about creation with imagination.

Is partnership to have a voice? Or will the Gospel be only "the throwing of a stone"? Will the heteronomous freedom of partnership in the Gospel—temporal, universal, loving, imaginative, and powerful—find a hearing? Or shall the determinists (both biblicist and materialist) win? Will your grandchildren sing the songs of freedom and grace? Or will a lockstep legalism of a purpose-driven life prevail? Hear the Gospel: *as a hen gathers her chicks . . .*

No, it is not too late for partnership. Abraham had a whole lot of nothing. And faith. And that gave him a future. Who knows what may come? Fifty-two years ago, I doubt that Marcia and Irving Hill thought that their misbehaving first baby, named Allan after Allan Knight Chalmers, would one day become the dean of Marsh Chapel. But here he is. It is not too late. The best time to plant an oak tree is one hundred years ago. The second best time is today.

We need one another. We need healthy partnerships: of learning and piety, of church and school, of school and university, of pulpit and lectern, of words and music, of lay and clergy, of women and men. To the partnership of the Gospel will we turn, for labor, in love, during the next decade. Will you respond? You are gathered here today for a reason—the partnership of the Gospel. Will you act?

Forgive me if I become quite specific, for a moment.

Voice, ethos, and hospitality cost.

Sermon by sermon this year, we have tried to announce a call to the ministry: our future voice. Sermon by sermon this year, we have tried to remember a charmed chapel story: our historical ethos. Sermon by

---

13. "There is a grandeur in this view of life, with its several powers, having been originally breathed into a few forms or into one; and that, whilst this planet has gone cycling on according to the fixed law of gravity, from so simple a beginning endless forms most beautiful and most wonderful have been, and are being, evolved." Darwin, *Origin of Species*, 425.

sermon this year, we have taught disciplined generosity: our chance at real hospitality.

We hope to complete the endowment of the Marsh Chapel deanship. Is there one person who would feel called to such a gift, in the partnership of the Gospel?

We hope to renovate this building. Are there a hundred people who would feel called to share the burden of such giving, in the partnership of the Gospel?

We hope to establish a Dempster House, an interreligous living unit for students (Hindu, Muslim, Jewish, Catholic, Protestant, Orthodox, all) committed to a common hope. Are there a thousand people who could share the burden of such a project, in the partnership of the Gospel?

Closing

We have provided personal counsel, and some solace, in this past week. One couple, reflecting on a grim tragedy, a loss of life and of friendship, sought counsel under the shadow of a familiar portrait. As we completed a prayer, the young man asked, "Who was Howard Thurman?" Before I could put into gear my own lengthy response, which like the peace of God would have passed all understanding and endured forever, his friend spoke. She answered, "Oh, I know his story: dean of Marsh Chapel, religious teacher, guide to Martin Luther King, advocate for a common ground . . ." In eight sentences, she had it. I still do not know which was more thrilling, his question or her answer!

Thurman wrote: "For this is why we were born: [People], all [people], belong to each other, and he who shuts himself away diminishes himself, and he who shuts another away from him destroys himself."[14]

Will you embrace the partnership of the Gospel?

---

14. Thurman, *Search for Common Ground*, 104. (Bracketed words reflect changes from gender-specific language found in the original.)

4

What a Friend We Have in . . . Paul

1 Corinthians 7:25–31
Delivered at Boston University Marsh Chapel
February 11, 2007

Paul—Apostle

WHAT A FRIEND WE have in Paul!

Paul—apostle whose mighty voice has rolled down through the ages bringing us the good news in all its stark simplicity: Christ the Lord is risen!

Paul—apostle raised in Tarsus, a Hebrew of the Hebrews, of the Tribe of Benjamin, as to the law a Pharisee, a defender of the traditions of the elders—and so a persecutor of the church.

Paul—apostle who rode to Damascus and on the way was blinded, and there heard a voice saying, "Saul, Saul, why persecutest thou me?"[1]

Paul—apostle who, in that blinding encounter with the Risen Lord, gave himself up, pronounced a sort of death sentence over himself, and so died with Christ and walked henceforth in newness of life.

Paul—apostle who believed that God had raised Jesus from the dead and so lived moment by moment, thinking, "Who knows what will happen next?"

---

1. Acts 9:4; 22:7; 26:14, KJV.

Paul—apostle who cared for those first few Christians, and worried about them, and grew angry with them, for they so easily lost this vision: that since God had raised Jesus from the dead, who knew what would happen next?

Paul's Apocalyptic World View

Paul—the apostle.

Who challenged the Thessalonians: "This is the will of God, your sanctification."[2]

Who challenged the Galatians: "Do not be deceived; God is not mocked."[3]

Who challenged the Philippians: "Live your life in a manner worthy of the gospel."[4]

Who challenged the Romans: "Do not be conformed to this age, but be transformed by the renewing of the mind."[5]

Who challenged the Corinthians: "Be reconciled."[6]

Paul—the apostle.

Whose mighty voice speaks to us today, ever answering the question of what we should do by saying something, first, about what God has done. Our faith springs not from ourselves but from God, the giver of both life and faith. "All religions are attempts to know God; none is the event of being known by God . . . God's graceful election of us by his rectifying and nonreligious invasion of the cosmos in Christ is the subject of the whole letter."[7]

Paul reminds us that "the present form of this world is passing away."[8] What else can we expect from a God who raises crucified Messiahs? Who knows what will happen next?

The future is as open as we, in faith, will allow it to be.

The voice of the Marsh Chapel pulpit, a national voice for a once vibrant, now wounded, nonetheless crucial form of faith—call it a responsible

---

2. 1 Thess 4:3, NRSVUE.
3. Gal 6:7, NRSVUE.
4. Phil 1:27, NRSVUE.
5. Rom 12:2, NRSVUE.
6. 2 Cor 5:20, NRSVUE.
7. Martyn, *Galatians*, 4:9.
8. 1 Cor 7:31, NRSVUE.

Christian liberalism—has not feared the future. We seek the truth, and so have nothing to defend and everything to share. So we may recognize, in this passage from 1 Corinthians 7, a form of thought that differs utterly from our own. If Paul did retain some of his formative Jewish worldview, the part he closely retained here was his inherited apocalyptic eschatology. The resurrection must be, he reasoned, the beginning of the end. Hence, preaches Paul, the form of this world is passing away.

Paul's worldview, his apocalyptic eschatology, is not our worldview. Paul's world, though, is very much ours, too. So we shall need to imagine, to dream, and to interpret these verses in a new way, for a new time.

Paul for a New Day

New occasions teach new duties. What a friend we have in the one non-gentile New Testament author who nonetheless was the "apostle to the gentiles"! Paul was a shirttail cousin of George Bernard Shaw, whose ringing question, "Why not?" haunts us. Paul was related, though not by marriage, to Robert Kennedy, who lived, in extremis, Shaw's question. Dr. James Walters of Boston University is a third cousin, twice removed in this lineage, for I did hear him say this week, in good Pauline fashion, "epiphanies are the vehicles through which God creates dreamers."

No, we may not share Paul's worldview, but we share his world. So we may benefit from his friendship, and practice his faith.

We may rely not on ourselves alone, but on God, who raises the dead.
We may face the world, free from the world.
We may lean into the future, free of the burden of past worry.
We can live on tiptoe.
We can compose every day with brilliance as if it were our last, which, in a way, each one is.

The person of faith, who overhears the distress down deep in this world, so deep that others don't hear it, does not rely on himself to soothe it. He knows there is one Savior, and he isn't him.

What a friend we have in Paul, who preaches "Jesus Christ, and him crucified."[9]

The Corinthians want to know about marriage.

Odd, strange, foreign, and alien as the teaching is to our ears, we must Paul attend. Says he: *don't worry, marriage isn't sinful.*

9. 1 Cor 2:2, NRSVUE.

An irrelevant answer to an unasked question, say we.

We never thought it was!

We forget Paul's apocalyptic worldview. We also forget that for Paul, and for many in earliest Christianity, marriage—as the epitome of dealings with "the world"—was decidedly inferior to celibacy. This text recommends a sort of brother/sister alliance. The early church so understood it. The desert father Amoun of Nitria (love that name) spent his honeymoon expounding 1 Corinthians 7 to his (surely puzzled) bride.

Why does Paul teach this way?

Because Paul expects that the form of this world is passing away. God has raised Jesus from the dead. Who knows what will happen next?

For Paul, this meant a daily, excited, imminent expectation of the turn of the ages, a new heaven and earth, the end of time and the beginning of a new era. For our sake, it is a blessing that Paul's own timeline was a little fuzzy; otherwise, we would not be here. But the spiritual truth that lives in this passage, its existential reality, is the same. Every day is our last. Paul so reminds us, and so shakes us out of our stupor. *This* is the day the Lord has made. We shall rejoice and be glad in it!

What if we are free?

What if Christ is risen?

What if the form of this world is passing away?

What if . . .

Our interest in the form of this world is so great that we don't notice the world that is to come. We forget. We rely upon ourselves when really, by faith, we mean to rely on God, who raises the dead. God who:

Has shown great strength with his arm.

Has scattered the proud in the imaginations of their hearts.

Has put down the mighty from their thrones.

Has exalted those of low degree.

In all of life, in the fullness of faith, there lies this strange, new potential. Potential. Potential for something new.

We face the world, free from the world.

We meet each day with courage.

We touch and are touched in the presence of divine potential, the raw possibility of a new day.

We live on tiptoe.

We live each day as if it were our last, which it is.

We greet the hour and its struggle from a certain distance, and over every loud booming statement there is a misty question mark.

This year at Marsh we have asserted that on a reliable hope hangs our future: a hope that life has meaning and that this world—not some gnostic netherworld but *this* world—can work. Weekly you have pressed: What are the features of this hope? We reply: one ingredient in hope is imagination, a willingness to live "as if not . . ."

As If Not . . . (One)

"As if not . . ."

The form of this world is passing away.

So, let those who have spouses live as if they had none. Let them be married, not in the form of this world, but in the form of the world to come, "as if not . . ."

Once there lived a model couple, pillars of church and community, who arrived at their midfifties in joyful wedlock. They were models of self-giving love. He would arise every morning thinking, "What can I do to make her life brighter today?" She would end every evening with some bright thought for the morning. The minister would pass by that house and smile.

Then one night, the preacher had a phone call from the couple, and a distressed question: "Can you come right over?" After some awkwardness and foot shuffling, they asked, "Would you marry us?" Well, it was a long story. Many years earlier, they had begun working together, running the town store. Times were tough, so, to save money, they moved in together. Then they fell in love. People in the town assumed they were married, and, well, what could they say? So, year followed year and decade followed decade. They felt, though, that was time to make it official. A simple, elegant ceremony ensued. The minister would pass by that house, again, with a smile.

About a month after the wedding, the minister received another late-night call. Down he went again to visit this model couple, who, for the first time, were on the verge of separation. They were at wits' end. The wife spoke up: "Nothing has been right since the wedding. It used to be, you know, every day was a new happiness. But since the ceremony and the ring and the certificate, I guess we have started to take each other for granted. There was something about being free to leave that kept both of us on our toes. We used to really watch out for each other, even serve each other. But now that the knot is tied, we are chafing at one another."

A long night of conversation followed. Tears and apologies, advice and consolation. There was a return of the old feeling for the old couple. In the wee hours, the minister put on his coat to leave. But before he left he forced the couple to make a solemn vow. He made them promise to live together, from that day forward, for better or worse, in sickness and in health, as if they were not married. As if not . . .

Let those who have spouses live as if they had none. Let us be married not in the form of this world but in that of the world to come. Not in complacency and disregard and a taking for granted—this world. But in surprise and kindness and joy and love—the world to come.

As If Not . . . (Two)

Let those who mourn do so as though they were not mourning. May they mourn not in the form of this world but in the form of the world to come.

A long time ago, up north, I called on woman in a nursing home, in the autumn of the year, in the autumn of her life. She was alone and was that day mourning the loss of her last living relative. Over tea, she made a familiar confession. "At eighteen, I knew everything there was to know. I had a tall pile of answers and hardly any questions. But somewhere between ages twenty-five and seventy-five, that pile began to shrink and another started to grow. Question jumped on top of question. Finally, about age eighty-five, I came to a point where I could honestly say I did not know anything, really, at all. With my sister gone, I know nothing and no one." Nothing? No one? She thought a little longer, and then added, with a gleam of contentedness shining through her deep hurt: "I guess I do know something and someone. I know him, whom I can trust."

There is something in that trust, that kind of proto-faith, which breathes with imagination. May our graduating seniors take heart! All the songs have not been sung yet. All the poems have not been written yet. The storehouse of good deeds yet undone has not closed for the evening.

My friend Jon Clinch, best man in our wedding and I in theirs, has a great new novel titled *Finn* coming out this month. The book imagines the life of Huckleberry Finn's father, Pap. Pap's life is something to be mourned, though his death is not. In the course of writing this dark tale, the author has given us an insight, a novel reading of the greatest American novel that no one, no one for a hundred and twenty years had earlier seen! You read this book and sense that the author has found the key to pick the lock of

Twain's mind! Do you know what a huckleberry is? What color it is? What hue? Twain hid his secret right in plain view, in the name, Huckleberry, whose mother, according to this newest fiction, was Black.

Let us imagine in the form of the world to come.

Let those who mourn do so as if they were not mourning, for the form of this world is passing away. When things go south, let us live not in the form of this world (in despair and doubt and dread), but in the form of the coming world (hope and freedom and a sense of God's awesome potential).

Paul has been read for two thousand years, yet only in the last generation was his apocalyptic eschatology fully appreciated. Paul awaited a new creation! How new? Look again, with J. L. Martyn, at the Greek text of Galatians 3:28, where Martyn finds an expectation of a new creation, so new that all the old categories, including those most debated today, are set aside:

> The variation in the wording of the last clause suggests that the author of the formula drew on Genesis 1:27, thereby saying that in baptism, the structure of the original creation had been set aside . . . it is a radical vision of loving mutuality enacted in the community of that new creation.[10]

Today, we mourn the loss of young life in Iraq. We read of the best and brightest, lost and lamented. Our hearts break. They break. Shall that mourning be our only mourning? Or shall we mourn the loss of the best and brightest in the form of the world to come? That is, with active imagination about what might honor their loss by preventing further loss?

As if not . . .

As If Not . . . (Three)

Let those who rejoice do so as if they were not rejoicing. Let them rejoice not in the form of this world but in the form of the world to come.

You know, it is not always clear what is bad news, or good. What can seem cause for the greatest rejoicing also can carry hurt, and vice versa. God's time is not our time. God's purpose is not equivalent to any one of ours. God's justice is not the same as our own. God's freedom far surpasses yours and mine. A crushing defeat can, in God's time, and with patience, become the source, the medium of great victory. I think of Franklin Roosevelt. Where would our country be today without his life's strange mixture

---

10. Martyn, *Galatians*, 3:28.

of rejoicing and suffering and struggle and perseverance? Is it not odd that the one president who appeared to be the least vigorous was in fact the most? As Cornel West would say: *To lead, you have to love; to save, you have to serve.*[11]

As If Not . . . (Four)

As if not . . .

Let those who buy and sell do so as if they had no goods. Not in the form of this world, but in the form of the world to come. Augustine said it so well: we use what we should love and we love what we should use.[12] We use people and love things when we are meant to love people and use things.

Let us allow Paul to befriend us. He may help us observe the reversals announced in Jesus's beatitudes. He may help us leave aside our negativity for the psalmist's "delight" in the Lord.

Said James Finley:

> Merton once told me to quit trying so hard in prayer. He said, "How does an apple ripen? It just sits in the sun." A small green apple cannot ripen in one night by tightening all its muscles, squinting its eyes and tightening its jaw in order to find itself the next morning miraculously large, red, ripe and juicy beside its small green counterparts. Like the birth of a baby or the opening of a rose, the birth of the true self takes place in God's time. We must wait for God, we must be awake; we must trust in his hidden action within us.[13]

Jesus told of a man who grew more and more crops and built bigger and bigger barns. At last the man could say: "Soul, . . . take thine ease, eat, drink, and be merry."[14] But that very night his soul was asked of him. "Then whose shall those things be?"[15]

Yes, use the things of this world, and buy and sell. Let us do so, though, not in the form of this world but in the form of the world to come. Not in grasping selfishness, not in anxious pursuit, not in such strangely intense

---

11. "You can't lead the people if you don't love the people. You can't save the people if you don't serve the people." West, *Hope on a Tightrope*, 151.
12. See: Augustine, *On Christian Doctrine*, 9.
13. Finley, *Merton's Palace of Nowhere*, 115-16.
14. Luke 12:19, KJV.
15. Luke 12:20, KJV.

attention. Rather: with aplomb, with a certain disregard, with an inner freedom.

About your car, your house, your wardrobe, your bank account, your things—ask this: Do you own it or does it own you? *Do you own it or does it own you?*

Coda

What a friend we have in Paul!
> Let those who have spouses live as if they had none;
> Those who mourn, as if not mourning;
> Those who rejoice, as if not rejoicing;
> Those who buy, as if not buying;
> Those who use this world, as if not using it,
> *For the form of this world is passing away.*

5

Two Songs of Solomon

Song of Solomon 2, 8, passim
John 3:1–11
Delivered at Boston University Marsh Chapel
February 17, 2008

Frontispiece

THERE ARE TWO SONGS of Solomon: one of the heart and one of the soul.
　　There are two Songs of Solomon: one of the flesh and one of the spirit.
　　There are two Songs of Solomon: one of earth and one of heaven.
　　There are two Songs of Solomon: one of human love and one of love divine.
　　There are two Songs of Solomon. Hear the Gospel: both are blessed!

> Three things are too wonderful for me;
> 　　four I do not understand:
> the way of an eagle in the sky,
> 　　the way of a snake on a rock,
> the way of a ship on the high seas,
> 　　and the way of a man and a woman.[1]

---

1. Prov 30:18-19, NRSVUE.

Faneuil Hall

In November, Jan and I rode the T to Haymarket Square with our daughter and our granddaughter. Our beloved's beloved baby gurgled past Boylston and Park. The Christmas lights glistened out from a soft *nevada*.[2] You could see your breath. Jan had seen advertised a free reading of love letters, from Abigail Adams to John Adams and from John Adams to Abigail Adams, offered in historic Faneuil Hall, and read by three couples named Patrick, Dukakis, and Kennedy.[3]

There are *kairos* moments. Whether or not your earnest study of Oscar Cullmann and Luke and Galatians convinces you, life will teach you. When Mrs. Patrick read Abigail's letter following Bunker Hill, to a distant John in Washington, full of terror and wonder at whether she would live the week, the air went out of the room. When Governor Dukakis read John's angry criticism of the laziness of the Congress, and paused midsentence to look meaningfully at Senator Kennedy, no words were needed to bring the house to robust laughter. When Kitty Dukakis read slowly the long love sentences, ripe and revealing, from wife to husband, from dearest friend to dearest friend, you wondered truly whether you could breathe again. When we heard the horrific sorrow of Abigail's mother's death, read out by Mrs. Kennedy, only a stone would not have cried. And I wonder about the stone. Every seat was full. As every heart. See how they loved each other!

Listen, for just a moment, Abigail to John: "That your Sex are Naturally Tyrannical is a Truth so thoroughly established as to admit of no dispute, but such of you as wish to be happy willingly give up the harsh title of Master for the more tender and endearing one of Friend."[4]

Listen for just a moment, John to Abigail: "It is a fortnight to day Since I had a Letter from you but it Seems to me a month. I cannot blame you for one of yours is worth four of mine."[5]

I say to our theology students: live in Boston. When your three years have passed, may you have spent two days in Boston for every one at

---

2. From Spanish: "snowfall."

3. The reading on November 19, 2007 was held to celebrate the publication of *My Dearest Friend: Letters of Abigail and John Adams* (Belknap, 2007). Several of the Adams's letters were read by former Massachusetts governor Michael Dukakis and Kitty Dukakis, then Massachusetts governor Deval Patrick and Diane Patrick, and then senator Edward Kennedy and Victoria Kennedy.

4. Adams and Adams, *My Dearest Friend*, 110.

5. Adams and Adams, *My Dearest Friend*, 370.

Boston University, two hours in the Copley Square library for every one at the School of Theology, two mornings in the Public Garden for every one at the student union, two nights with the Celtics and Red Sox for every one watching TV in the apartment, two meals in the North End for every one in the Back Bay, two winter afternoons walking on Commonwealth for every one in the campus gym, two desserts on Newbury Street for every one at home.

If I never have another such *kairotic* moment in Boston, this one evening will have been enough. To whomever arranged such a rhetorical explosion, I offer belated thanksgiving. There is such power, such a searing power, in public reading, in public reading of hallowed words, in public reading of hallowed words fitly spoken. You pick up and read, and read aloud, *My Dearest Friend*, and judge for yourself. It brings to mind a little-remembered verse from a maverick book in the Bible, which itself is a testament of freedom.

"Love is [as] strong as death."[6] That sentence appears in the Song of Solomon. But, for those with eyes to see and ears to hear, there are really two songs of Solomon, and both are blessed.

Heart

One Solomon song sings of human love. And how it sings! So loud it sings, and so dearly and strong that the sages in Jamnia nearly excluded it from the canon!

You will have your choicest choices. Here are two:

> Arise, my love, my fair one,
>   and come away,
> for now the winter is past,
>   the rain is over and gone.
> The flowers appear on the earth;
>   the time of singing has come,
> and the voice of the turtledove
>   is heard in our land.[7]
>
> How beautiful you are, my love,
>   how very beautiful!

---

6. Song 8:6, NRSVUE.
7. Song 2:10–12, NRSVUE.

Your eyes are doves
    behind your veil.
Your hair is like a flock of goats,
    moving down the slopes of Gilead.
Your teeth are like a flock of shorn ewes . . .
    . . .
Your lips are like a crimson thread . . .
    . . .
Your cheeks are like halves of a pomegranate . . .
    . . .
[You can read the rest yourself!!]
    . . .
You are altogether beautiful, my love;
    there is no flaw in you.[8]

Collected in the Canticles[9] are love poems, erotic poems, poems of praise for human love. One of our members asked a year ago whether any sermons are ever preached on the Song. The implication was that the verses are simply too hot to handle! Last week, another member related that in childhood, advised to read the Bible, she had stumbled into these verses. I believe she said: "Wow!"

Saddled with other challenges for a few decades, the historic church may have lost of some of our voice about love, human love, sexuality, human sexuality, and the ardent themes of the Song of Songs, the meta-song of the Hebrew Scripture. While our own straitened conditions in the church and our inwardly turned attention to the details of liturgy may constrain us, all about us the culture calls out for the good news of these chapters. *It is still the same old story.*

The stories of Alistair MacLeod, Canadian celebrant of life, are ever reaching for the misty and mystic heights of the Song of Solomon. MacLeod, with the exception of one passing humorous reference to an inept clergyman, in none of his published material makes any reference to God, Christ, Spirit, Church, religion, faith, belief, or Bible. Like the Song of Solomon, he never mentions God. Yet his work, to my ear, proffers some of the strongest theological reflection of our time. *Island*,[10] his stories, and *No*

---

8. Song 4:1–7, NRSVUE.
9. The Song of Songs is also called the Canticle of Canticles or the Song of Solomon.
10. McClelland and Stewart, 2000.

Great Mischief,[11] his novel, teem with love. He compares one Cape Breton couple to eagles, who mate for life and soar to the heights.

The verses of the Song of Songs may have arisen as wedding songs. They celebrate love leading toward marriage and love established in marriage, without a great deal of distinction between the two. They acknowledge the power of love. They drape their music in the imagery of the natural world. They shout for joy for the joyful shout of love, human love. As a pastor, father, friend, now minister to a university community, I might have wished a little more didactic material had found its way into the Canticle. A little admonition about commitment. A little recognition of selfishness. A little sober admission of imperfection. A little paternal warning about regret and regrets. Well, we shall have to find these in other pages of the Scripture, for these songs are flying to other places. They reflect the human experience of the ages. They delight in delight. They delight in delight!

Yes, I could interpret and amend these passages to make sure that we include partnership and friendship as well as covenant and marriage. Yes, we could dwell for a moment on the difference between the literature here and that in the rest of the Bible—there is no overt religious content corresponding to the other books of the Bible.[12] Yes, I could remember the sectarian Jewish warning that the book should only be opened and read after age thirty. Yes, I could reflect on what emptiness of the soul does, on this weekend following the further campus tragedy at Northern Illinois. Yes, I could present to the contrary T. Wolfe's sad narrative *I Am Charlotte Simmons*.[13] For those teaching and learning in a large, historically Methodist university, it bears reading. We use when we should love and vice versa. Thus, though, I would miss the point. The Song of Solomon sings of blessing!

Human love is blessed.

---

11. McClelland and Stewart, 1999.

12. "The Song of Songs is a collection of love songs that do not have the least intent of symbolizing divine love, nor have they derived from pagan religious celebrations . . . It is in subject matter that the Song diverges sharply from most extant pre-Christian Jewish literature." Gottwald, "Song of Songs," 424.

13. Farrar, Straus and Giroux, 2004.

Soul

But there are two Songs of Solomon: one of heart and one of soul, one of flesh and one of spirit, one of earth and one of heaven, one of human love and one of love divine.

Another Solomon song sings of love divine.

The allegorical, cultic, dramatic, and other nonliteral readings of the Song of Solomon have less influence today. In any case, they fall fairly quickly in the face of the ardent, strong sensuality of the collection. The rabbis early allegorized the Song to refer to Yahweh and Israel. The early church followed suit, and allegorized the Song to refer to Christ and the Church, or to God and the soul. Hosea had already used the allegory, in his beautiful chapters, the eleventh being perhaps the loveliest in Scripture. But he had done so forthrightly, intending and intoning the allegory directly. "When Israel was a child, I loved him."[14] As a reading of the text, it must be said today, that the allegory superimposes something not apparent or present.

What is dethroned from Scripture, however, experience re-crowns. It is not without wisdom that this bit of wisdom literature has been taken to refer, in a Lenten fashion, to the love of the soul for God, to the love of God for the soul, to the love of the church for Christ, to the love of Christ for the church. After all, how are we ever going to picture, to propose the relationship of the human being to God?

Here is today's gospel message:

What can prepare us for intimacy with the divine, if not human intimacy?

What can prepare us for covenant with the divine, if not human covenant?

What can prepare us for fellowship with the divine, if not human fellowship?

What can prepare us for love of the divine, if not human love?

Where else are we going to learn the rhythms of relationship that prepare a community and its individuals, an individual and their communities, for ultimate relationship?

No wonder Plato wrote so tenderly and toughly about friendship. No wonder John the Evangelist epitomized discipleship in the portrait of one "beloved." No wonder Bernard of Clairvaux wrote eighty-six sermons on the Song of Songs and never got past the second chapter! No wonder that

---

14. Hos 11:1, NRSVUE.

John of the Cross and Teresa of Ávila formed their religious poetry on the model of love poetry. No wonder that even today there is a returning interest in "nuptial mysticism," a recognition that love, friendship, partnership, marriage shape a soulful habit of living. It is in the relationship of lover and beloved that we plumb the depths of experience.

In relationship, we are addressed, truly, from beyond ourselves. We are forced, in real relationship, daily, to face our limitations. We are, in relationship, known, personally, underneath the public masks. We are tested, interpersonally, regarding our patience, stamina, endurance, perseverance, long-suffering, and grace under pressure. We are surprised by joy. Joy in love. Joy in creation. Joy in communion. Joy in devotion. Morning and evening, we are surprised by joy. Even C. S. Lewis, no non-traditionalist he, could find the epitome of his orthodoxy in an astounding marriage and friendship and love with Joy.

My friend and student Joshua Duncan, relying on our colleague Phil Wogaman, helped me research this sermon. Joshua wrote:

> Bernard preached dozens of sermons and wrote volumes on the Song. There is an entire sermon just on "Let him kiss me with the kisses of his mouth,"[15] so it is hard to synthesize. I hope this will suffice.
>
> Bernard used the Song to form an ethic based on love. Love, he felt, allowed people to transform from our natural fallen and selfish state to a more holy state. This happens in stages. First, love is for self, and love of God in the first stage is for the sake of one's self. But this is not an improper love, because it allows for movement to stage two. This happens when we realize our own limitations, and desire to transcend them. Stage two is love of God for what he gives us (namely, grace). Once we move beyond our limitations (Bernard is a mystic), we are able to enter stage three, love of God for God's own sake, even to the extent of forgetting ourselves. In stage four, we love ourselves once again, but it is an emptied out version of ourselves (did someone say mysticism?). The love of ourselves in stage four is entirely unselfish, because it is a love of ourselves purely for the sake of God.[16]

In the mountains northwest of Madrid, you will find nestled the little old Castilian village of Segovia.

---

15. Song 1:2, NRSVUE.
16. Duncan, personal correspondence with author, 2008.

I spent only a year there. I walked its cobbled streets during the evening *paseo*. I was befriended by its teenagers. Adios, Roberto. Adios, Marie Carmen. Adios, Celia. Adios, Eduardo. I gazed out at the mountain range that had inspired Hemingway. I ate the baked lamb and drank the red wine of that region. I admired its aqueduct. I photographed its castle. I learned the language, the humor, the humors, the history, the heart, the soul of a noble people. I walked in the dark late-night rain and greeted the town crier and constable: "Adios." Someday, I hope to return. I find that Segovia appears with more regularity in my dreams now than it has for the thirty years past.

I visited there the resting place of Saint John of the Cross. I read and remembered his poetry:

> *En una noche oscura,*
> *con ansias en amores inflamada*
> *¡o dichosa ventura!*
> *salí sin ser notada,*
> *estando ya mi casa sosegada.*[17]

Lent may not seem like the right time to read the Song of Songs. Yet it is the perfect time! Our hearts are restless, restless, until they find their rest in the divine, the second song of Solomon. Such a word of longing! Is there anything, any theme more Lenten than that of longing!?!

> Set me as a seal upon your heart,
>   as a seal upon your arm,
> for love is strong as death,
>   passion fierce as the grave.
> Its flashes are flashes of fire,
>   a raging flame.
> Many waters cannot quench love,
>   neither can floods drown it.
> If one offered for love
>   all the wealth of one's house,
>   it would be utterly scorned.[18]

Human love is blessed—by God.

---

17. "In a dark night, / With anxious love inflamed, / O, happy lot! / Forth unobserved I went, / My house being now at rest." John of the Cross, "Noche oscura del alma" ["The Dark Night of the Soul"], st. 1.

18. Song 8:6-7, NRSVUE.

Invitation

There are two Songs of Solomon.

In earshot of the two Songs of Solomon—love divine and human, both—*let me invite you to a better life.*

Let me invite you to cherish friendship, and to bathe friendship, like a lover, in the warm baths of time and attention. Let me invite you to honor partnership, and to bathe partnership, like a lover, in the warm baths of time and attention. Let me invite you to enjoy affection, and to bathe affection, like a lover, in warm baths of time and attention. Let me invite you to revere marriage, and to bathe marriage, like a lover, in the warm baths of time and attention.

For such friendship may frame your soul in communion with the divine. Such partnership may prepare your soul for commerce with the divine. Such affection may prepare your psyche for intimacy with the divine. Such marriage may open you . . . to God.

> "For love is strong as death,
>   passion fierce as the grave."[19]

---

19. Song 8:6, NRSVUE.

6

Merrywood

Mark 10:17–31
Delivered at Boston University Marsh Chapel
October 11, 2009

IN THE EARLY PART of August, 2009, the newspaper, our national "paper of record," carried a front-page article about a tragic accident in Upstate New York. Many months earlier, near Auburn, New York, a bright young college freshman, a creative, itinerant musician, by accident ran his motorcycle headlong into a car that was waiting for oncoming traffic to turn. For six months he was, as the article reported, "a vegetable" at twenty years of age.

Not far from the location of this tragic accident in Upstate New York, more than thirty years ago, I had made my first official pastoral visit. The hospital was located near Auburn. The young man, age twenty, had been in a motorcycle accident, too. He too survived, but with his life forever altered. His one hope had been to become a New York state trooper, and his chances had been good prior to his own accident. Now, with his injuries, he would not qualify. Devastated would be an understated description of his condition. I see that young man in my mind's eye almost every time I make a hospital call or another visit, an average of twenty-five calls per week over these thirty-two years (an instructional aside for seminarians). Also, fifteen years ago, I briefly became the district superintendent designate (a church administrative role) in the area of the tragic accident. I accepted because of the people I had known in the office, who were honorable and bright, who had helped me, who were genuine preachers and pastors.

Returning to the present. Our young motorcyclist whose story was told last summer suffered massive brain injury. For six months he lay in a vegetative state. Over the following six months only minimal improvement occurred. His family waited on him hand and foot and diaper. His younger brother spent large swaths of every day with him. But he could not recognize his own mother. "Who are you?" Think about that for a moment. His brother would get so desperate that he would lift the young man and drop him to floor, shouting to be recognized, shouting to make himself heard. Shouting at the top of his lungs to wake his beloved sibling from mortal sleep.

Since 1986 I have been shouting myself, but about another tragedy. In prayer, in sermons, in books, in lectures, in speeches, in articles, in conversation, in debate, on the blog. Shouting. "Wake up! Wake up! Thou Rip Van Winkle in the land of Rip Van Winkle! Wake up!"

After about a year comatose, the young man began to revive. He still has no memory and no forecasting perspective. He spends his days in a group home, taking walks, visiting the zoo and the county fair, walking past the green lawns of the college in which he was once enrolled. Think about it for a moment. A tragic accident strips you of health, of mind, of memory, of identity, and nearly kills you. In fact, to some degree, or by some measure, you may be dead (see Luke 15).

The newspaper of record reported on the upstate accident, in part, because healing came to our young cyclist.

His healing came not by means of surgery or medication or other attention to the massive damage his frontal lobe, his main brain, sustained. The article meanders endlessly regarding how many and what types of attempts were so made. To no avail. His only partial, and very gradual, renewal came—by another way. When the main roads of the brain have been washed out, or bombed out, or obliterated otherwise, the brain turns to the back roads. Healing comes indirectly. Healing comes from the little capillaries. Healing comes from the country paths, the little lanes, the overgrown and unmapped and even unplowed blue highways of the brain. The superhighways are left behind, to atrophy, age, weaken, and collapse. The blood flows backward, not exactly uphill, but outback. The blood finds other little routes by which to nourish the barren brain. And some grudging, slow, partial, painstaking healing arrives.

My church, the United Methodist Church of the Northeastern Jurisdiction, was riding high on a motorcycle some forty years ago when there was a tragic accident. Half the membership disappeared. The remaining half became twice as old. The buildings aged double-time, with little maintenance as some sanctuary roofs collapsed. Administratively inexperienced leadership was empowered. Simple truths—about inclusiveness, choice, peace, reason, truth—were forgotten. Support and salaries withered. Uneducated preachers occupied half the pulpits. Buildings were sold, campgrounds closed, missions aborted, youth groups eclipsed. The one great feature of our branch of Protestantism, choral singing in four part harmony, was displaced by happy clappy, Jesus is my girlfriend, follow the bouncing ball, one-line blast music. Energetic, intelligent, aggressive, ambitious young people found other vocations than preaching. My church hit a car and catapulted downhill to brain damage, lost memory, forgotten identity and near death, or a kind of death. The membership of the New England Conference, on the day of that metaphorical collision, was two hundred ten thousand; today, it is eighty thousand. New Jersey: two hundred thousand, now eighty-five thousand. North Central New York: one hundred fifty-five thousand, now sixty thousand. Troy and Wyoming: one hundred twenty thousand, now forty-five thousand. Church meetings, in the few cases that they involved conference—that is, a chance to confer in honest and kind conversation—pitted those committed to rebuilding the church against those committed to opening up the church. Build or open up? Build or open up? Those were the options, with little but a glimmer of memory that one requires the other.

The foremost current historian of Methodism asked me, in 2004, if I thought the UMC had any future. I gave my reply, and he returned the favor. "No," he said.

Like a brother I have shouted. Like a brother I have lifted and dropped. Like a brother I have cared and loved. Some of you have, too. But the cerebral cortex changeth not.

The week after the article appeared about the tragic accident and the unexpected healing in Upstate New York, my granddaughter and grandson and I, along with their parents, strolled in the village of my upbringing. A bucolic setting for a lifetime of sermonic *bildungsromanic* material surrounded me there, as it does on every visit to the farmers' Saturday market.

Jan later said, piercingly, how much growing up in the little college town of Hamilton, New York, had forged my self. A love of free space, and freedom to move around save and unhindered. A familiarity with and confidence in academia. An assumption about the certain goodness of the church as one part, only one part, of God's good community. A regard, early and late, for the quality of speech, the significance of language, the joyful love of the mother tongue. A joy in fishing, hiking, swimming, skiing, skating, cycling, golfing, all at the drop of a hat, all within a ten-minute ride or twenty-minute walk. No oversight, and the recognition of the freedom in such freedom. Time and space for friendship without the intrusions on friendship that come with wealth. A long twilight childhood, for which twilight did not fall and the streetlights did not come on until age thirteen and the mudslide of Woodstock and the mudslide of American culture.

That day I took my son in law to see the Methodist Church. With his children we walked around to the back of the church. Once there had been a simple lawn there, like the many and simple lawns that lushly and lavishly adorn so many of the Upstate cities and towns. I remembered the side street as a dirt road, but it was now paved. Behind the church there is a playground. I want to describe it for you. Here is the reason I want to describe it for you: it is a capillary, a little vessel carrying a little blood, a tiny moment of real healing coming out of the back roads by the rivers of memory, ever smiling, ever gentle on the mind.

The playground is named "Merrywood." It is an example of spirit, speech, and space making way for a common grace. "Merrywood: A toddler park, in the spirit of community," says the sign. Welcome. The donors are listed. Some are Methodists from the church whose lawn holds Merrywood. Some are neighbors, who have lived in that location for sixty years. One is in memory of such a neighbor, who died as the park was built. The Rotary Club joined the partnership. And there is the church, presumably absorbing exposure, responsibility, liability, and insurance.

As one who was a child on that backstreet, that back lane, I found the sign on the fence breathtaking. Listen to its simple sentences:

> Welcome to Merrywood.
> There is a child in all of us, but this playground is for children.
> On Sunday mornings, we prefer praying to playing. During services, you are welcome to join us inside.
> Our neighbors love children, but they also enjoy quiet mornings and quiet evenings.
> Narrow little John Street is perfect for walking, but not for parking.

Toddlers, please make sure your adult friend stays and plays with you at all times. Don't let them sneak away.

Not: ADOLESCENTS STAY OUT. CLOSED ON SUNDAY MORNING. STAY OUT BEFORE 9 AND AFTER 8. NO PARKING. CHILDREN MUST BE SUPERVISED AT ALL TIMES.

Rather: graceful, playful admonition and reminder, a gentleness in discourse and so in community.

There will be no large, lasting, quick recovery for the UMC of the NEJ. The time to have attempted that was before the boat had started fully to capsize, before our cycle crash. Our last real chance came about twenty years ago (humanly speaking, of course). The massive damage to the main brain, the catastrophic near lobotomy of the cerebral cortex, will not directly be healed. But there are the back roads, the capillaries, the little vessels, the Merrywoods.

Merrywood models spirit. Those who built the playground in 2003 (one assumes with the pastoral imagination of the minister leading the way) had about them a certain spirit. A humble spirit. A human spirit, or a humanizing one. A readiness to admit that there are many ways to keep faith. An openness to others, especially to unknown, different, future, foreign others. A care for children, the least of these. A modest mode of partnership, Methodist and Baptist, town and gown, Rotary and church, neighbor and visitor, one generation to another. Our future will also bear the mark, the imprint of this spirit (see Galatians 5:22). There is, here, a memory that ministry is service. There is, here, a memory that ministry includes children. There is, here, a memory that Jesus was the person for others, and that the church is the community of faith working through love. There is a memory that it is God who heals, and we are his, the sheep of his pasture. "Love is God." You might say that there is a Christological memory at work, battling the Christological amnesia of the last forty years. (The Gospel of Mark, including our reading today, has something to say about Christological amnesia.) And, to be clear—to say it so that there is no mistaking it—there is a memory, here, of grace. Merrywood is a reflection of a common grace, the partnership of the gospel (see Philippians 1:3). But that memory starts with grace prevenient, prevenient grace. Before we hear of it, God is at work, loving children, speaking kindly, opening space for common grace. Those who built Merrywood, perhaps mutely but truly nonetheless, affirmed faith in prevenient grace. Our healing comes across such back roads. Unexpected, common grace!

Merrywood models speech. How something is said is just as important as what is said. There are flat, fundamental, and finally false ways of saying things that are the equivalent of shouting at a hearing-impaired person. With every occasion for communication, including the very simplest, as evidenced in the Merrywood sign, there is an opportunity for grace. We have very little left to go on, we in the Protestant church in the Northeast. A few thousand sixty-year-old members, a few hundred hundred-and-fifty-year-old churches, a few scraps of memory. But people instinctively hear good news. They know when the gospel has been preached. They hear it. They feel it. They know it in their bones. People who read the Merrywood sign know they are being addressed, if they allow themselves to be at all addressable, from another realm, a dominion of grace, a just, justified, justifying, rightwising, loving, freeing realm of grace. I repeat the gracious admonitions. Listen to the way they are put:

> *Welcome to Merrywood.*
> *There is a child in all of us, but this playground is for children.*
> *On Sunday mornings, we prefer praying to playing. During services, you are welcome to join us inside.*
> *Our neighbors love children, but they also enjoy quiet mornings and quiet evenings.*
> *Narrow little John Street is perfect for walking, but not for parking.*
> *Toddlers, please make sure your adult friend stays and plays with you at all times. Don't let them sneak away.*

This is not nostalgia, not flummery, not rhetorical trimming, not cute speech. It is a moment of justifying grace. The writer, or speaker, is not worried, is not anxious, and does not have a furrowed brow. The speaker is not a salesman, but a witness. The speaker does not need a certain response. Another world, a new creation, is peeking in upon the dementia of a dying church within the loneliness of a frightened world. Here we are, she says! Come in! Play! Enjoy! Oh, and if you are so moved, come and enjoy, come Sunday, what means most to us. It is that indirection, telling the truth but telling it slant[1] (as the poet said), that confident aplomb, that air of happy courage that is everything, justifying grace, gospel. If we are to speak the gospel, we shall need Merrywood speech, just grace, a willingness to lay down our sword and shield, to put on a long white robe, to study verbal war no more.[2] If, that is, we want to be heard by a world that increasingly

---

1. Dickinson, "Tell all the truth but tell it slant—," no. 1263.
2. "I ain't gonna study war no more" is a repeated chorus line in the African-American

experiences language as aerial bombardment and hit-and-run driving and other forms of e-damage. Those who planned Merrywood affirmed, perhaps indirectly but nonetheless truly, their sturdy faith in grace that justifies, on its own terms. Healing comes across such forgotten, overgrown, unplowed back roads.

Merrywood models space. Those who imagined and created this remarkable play space did so with a certain eye upon space. Read, sometime, Gaston Bachelard's *Poetics of Space*.[3] Children who grow up in high broad space have a high broad perspective. Setting the spatial setting is 90 percent of education.

Now, we want to become very practical for a moment. Across the UMC of the NEJ we lack many things. You make your list. Here is mine. We lack: leadership, money, trust, skill, memory, courage, numbers, heart. But there is one thing of which we have almost endless supply: space. Unused, empty, vacated churches, lawns, buildings, lots, land, space. Space, we got. So, why not use it *for the common grace?* Why not take empty churches and make Merrywoods? Have we forgotten the love we had at first? There is hardly a setting in our conferences that, with a little pastoral imagination, could not become a Merrywood, small or large. All eight churches that Jan and I have served, over time and distinctly and in some way, have done so. Life is not about what you do not have (see Exodus 20). It is about what you do have. Enjoy what you have. Do what you can. Be who you are. Well, we do have space. One church could use its empty sanctuary to provide sanctuary for Iraqi refugees. Another could use its forlorn basement for LGBTQ ministry. One church could use its lawn for skating rinks and hockey. Another church could use its garret to house unemployed members. And so on. Those who built Merrywood exhibited, however mutely or unconsciously, a confidence, a faith in sanctifying grace, in the possibility, by back roads, of betterment. You can if you think you can. That is not a word about spirit. That is not a word about speech. That is word about space.

Later last summer, I heard our daughter and son-in-law singing to both children as they were bathed. "This little light of mine . . . This is the day . . . I love the mountains, I love the rolling hills . . . Every round goes higher higher . . ."

---

spiritual "Down by the Riverside" (first published 1918); other stanzas include the lines: "Gonna lay down my sword and shield" and "Gonna try on my long white robe."

3. Beacon, 1994.

When these children sing the songs of faith, like "This is the day," I feel happy, and more, I feel some hope. Their parents, clergy they, are not going to give over the church, the broad, magnanimous, open, liberal, large, loving, free, caring Christian church, to the fears of religionists. They know the difference, and they live it.

Healing is coming. Slowly. Partially. Painfully. Indirectly. Along the back roads. In spirit. In speech. In space. Grace prevenient—spirit. Grace justifying—speech. Grace sanctifying—space.

Welcome to Merrywood . . .

7

Remembering Howard Thurman

John 10:22–30
Delivered at Boston University Marsh Chapel
Second Annual Marsh Chapel Thurman Day Student Service: April 25, 2010

Two Approaches to Christ in John 10

TWO STARTLING, CONFLICTING APPROACHES to Christ accost us in our Scripture lesson this morning. One, the presence. Two, the shepherd. It may be that you, of a sudden, this hour, will find your way forward, walking hand in hand, presence to the left, shepherd to the right. You may find you need a hand one day. W. S. Coffin: "It is often said that the Church is a crutch. Of course it's a crutch. What makes you think you don't limp?"[1]

Our verses were born—hear the coached breathing, the contractions, the shouts of pain—in distress. We shall suppose the following setting: the year, 100 BCE; the place, Ephesus; the audience, a small, fierce, and fledgling church; the cast, a group of people who have been thrown out of their community at just the moment that they have lost their main belief. They have lost belonging and meaning in the same breath of contraction. That is, they once happily affirmed Jesus in the synagogue. But that lasted only as long as they were traditionally monotheistic. Once the Spirit said of Jesus, "The

---

1. Coffin, *Credo*, 137.

Father and I are one,"[2] they had to pack their bags. To grow up, they had to leave home. In the same years—I prize the courageous honesty of these early relatives of yours—they had to face up to the fact that Jesus was not coming back, in the manner of the primitive hope, any time soon. The great, primary apocalyptic hope of the primitive church—"with a cry of command, with the archangel's call and with the sound of God's trumpet"[3]—proved false. *Parousia* gave way to Paraclete, Armageddon to the artistry of every day, and speculation to Spirit. Necessity once again gave birth to newness. They had to open the door and unshutter the window, to broaden their religious circle and open their spiritual perspective. You need to feel your way into a moment in life—yours or another's—in which your community of friends is wrecked and your sense of purpose is destroyed.

For instance, in these days and weeks, we embrace those about to graduate.

As you participate in various community gatherings, and then are cast out or cast out into the real world, you may have occasion to recall the Scriptural witness today to similar experience.

What we hear in John 10 is a sermon, or part of one. You may wonder why modern sermons are not limited to eight verses—well, things do not always get better! Motion is not progress. In this sermon, delivered seventy years after the crucifixion, an explanation of disappointment and dislocation (remember, no apocalypse and no community of origin) is affirmed, to help people. Preaching is meant to help people. To know Christ is to know his benefits. We are out in the snowbank, de-communitized, for a reason, says the preacher. Jesus in Paraclete said: "The Father and I are one." But for the traditional monotheists among us, this presents a problem. One, we got. Two? Not so much. And we haven't even raised the Trinity issue, the move to three, yet. So it is time to move, to itinerate, to know again the lostness of being outside, starting over, existential commencement.

But. Jesus in Paraclete also says something else. Your greatest freedom may, surprisingly, be embedded in your most hurtful disappointment. Your truest grace may, surprisingly, be embedded in your most wrenching dislocation. That door, once opened—that window, once unshuttered—offers a clean breeze and warm sunlight.

---

2. John 10:30, NRSVUE.
3. 1 Thess 4:16, NRSVUE.

We move to commencement, a new beginning, honoring our graduates, singing freedom into the maw of disappointment, singing grace into the cavernous maw of dislocation.

At least, that is what John's little community discovered, and called eternal life, resurrection, salvation, truth. You didn't need that tight-knit community after all. You didn't need that superannuated hope after all. Because *the sheep know the shepherd's voice.*

> My life flows on in endless song;
> Above earth's lamentation,
> I catch the sweet though far-off hymn
> That hails a new creation.
> . . .
> No storm can shake my inmost calm,
> While to that refuge clinging;
> Since Christ is Lord of heaven and earth,
> How can I keep from singing?[4]

Two Christs: one transcendent, one immanent, one divine, one human, one silent, one shepherd. "The Father and I are one." "My sheep hear my voice."[5] There is nothing more personal than voice. Not fingerprint, not DNA, not Facebook catchalls. Voice is the personal given life. Hence, preaching, the sacrament of preaching. Romans 10:17: "Faith comes from what is heard." I wonder whether you are deep enough in disappointment and dislocation to bump into freedom and grace? Every sermon, in almost every religious tradition, is a call to decision, a dualism of decision: a call to personal loving and giving, a call to communal giving and loving, a call to relational authority and authentic relationship, a call to service and care.

Our Day Today and Two Christological Perils

Our son Ben said once of his grandfather, "I love to hear his voice." Last year, his grandfather[6] survived a nearly mortal illness. There are not words to convey the joy, the gratitude, that we his family experience in his escape. Those who have been on the brink of death can appreciate 10:28: "I give them eternal life, and they will never perish. No one will snatch them

---

4. Hartley, "My Life Flows On," no. 279, st. 1 and 2.
5. John 10:27, NRSVUE.
6. Rev. Mr. Irving G. Hill (1928–2010; BUSTH '53).

out of my hand."⁷ Not all such deliverance has an earthly horizon. Some freedom and some grace must await us across the river—and I don't mean Harvard—but some comes to us here. My father and mother lived here in Boston from 1950 to 1953. In 1975, he wrote the following sentences in the back of a book. I quote them with permission.

> The temptation for the people of the church in every age is to believe: a) Jesus is only human; b) Jesus only appeared to be human. For those who settle on "a," there is no power, no mystery, no pull to pry them out of much of life. For those who choose "b," there is no hope, because mankind cannot ascend the heights of divinity. Both are heresies. The pious wise men of AD 325 saw, though they could not explain it, that he was fully human and fully divine.⁸

They departed Boston in 1953, just as Howard Thurman came to town. Rev. Gomes last week recalled, as he and I exchanged pulpits, that George Buttrick and Howard Thurman used to do the same. Thurman's voice carries us into two dimensions, two realms of reality. He was one hundred years ahead of his time fifty years ago (my standard way of introducing Thurman), so he is still fifty years ahead of you (and me). He evoked the Christ of Common Ground, transcendent, universal, shared, unconfined, free. He evoked the Christ of the Disinherited, immanent, particular, grasped, embodied, back against the wall. Two Christs. One and Shepherd. Calling out to you to know the grain of your own wood, not to cut against the grain of your own wood . . .

Our six ministry associates prepared this sermon, in three hours of mortal combat with me, and three hours of cultural and biblical exegesis, confronting John 10 and April 25. They turned for support to Howard Thurman. To his book *The Search for Common Ground*.⁹ To his book, *Jesus and the Disinherited*.¹⁰ You can, too. But they as a group vehemently argued against processed religion. "It's worse for you than processed food," they said. "I like Wonder Bread," I objected. So they had to teach me to beware processed food and beware processed religion. They showed me a video called "I am Sorry I am a Christian." They confessed, "Even though Easter has come, it does not always feel that way." Late April means more normal liturgy, a coming move out of the dorms (talk about dislocation), new life

---

7. John 10:28, NRSVUE.
8. Hill, personal correspondence with author, 1975.
9. Harper and Row, 1971.
10. Abingdon-Cokesbury, 1949.

and growth, but also old and enduring challenges. Hear they are, in voice: our 2010 Marsh Chapel Ministry Associates, lifting again Thurman's *Common Ground* and Thurman's *Disinherited*.

Thurman and Transcendence: *The Search for Common Ground*

> I am Kelly Drescher, Ministry Associate on the Medical Campus. Our work across campus this year has involved us in many individual lives and many forms of ministry, both with religious and with unreligious people. We have striven to bring a sense of freedom and grace to all, to recognize the "common ground" upon which we walk. As Thurman wrote in *The Search for Common Ground*, the creation myth of the Hopi Indians carries still, in its thematic emphasis on "the memory of a lost harmony."[11]
>
> I am Jenn Quigley, Ministry Associate for Student Affairs. Thurman wrote of a unity of living structures that includes rocks, plants, animals, and humans. Antibodies and antigens. And the arrangement of a cell in a human child.[12]
>
> I am Lauren Miramontes, Ministry Associate for the Interfaith Council. Thurman cites Plato: "Until philosophers are kings . . . and political greatness and wisdom meet in one, and those commoner natures who pursue either to the exclusion of the other are compelled to stand aside, cities will never have rest from their evils."[13]

In the voice of Howard Thurman, a hundred years ahead of his time fifty years ago, there is a regard for mystery, silence, presence, the transcendent, where Jesus the Paraclete can say, "The Father and I are one." One in kinship with all of creation. One in kinship with every human being, so that nothing human is foreign to us. One in transformative engagement with the soup of our natural world, our home, our condition, our circumstance. One in openness to the great differences and diversities of personal—that is to say, religious—expression, including myth from long ago and far away.

The presence.

---

11. Thurman, *Common Ground*, 23.

12. Thurman, *Common Ground*. See esp. chap. 3, "The Search in Living Structures," 29–41.

13. Thurman, *Common Ground*, 49.

Thurman and Immanence: *Jesus and the Disinherited*

I am Micah Christian, Ministry Associate for First Year Students [our fourth, he follows Augie Delbert in 2009, David Romanik in 2008, and Larry Whitney in 2007]. "Jesus rejected hatred. It was not because he lacked the vitality or the strength. It was not because he lacked the incentive. Jesus rejected hatred because he saw that hatred meant death to the mind, death to the spirit, death to communion with his Father. He affirmed life, and hatred was the great denial."[14]

I am Soren Hessler, Ministry Associate in Judicial Affairs. "There is something more to be said about the inner equipment growing out of the great affirmation of Jesus that a man is a *child* of God. If a man's ego has been stabilized, resulting in a sure grounding of his sense of personal worth and dignity, then he is in a position to appraise his own intrinsic powers, gifts, talents, and abilities. He no longer views his equipment through the darkened lenses of those who are largely responsible for his social predicament."[15]

I am John Prust, Ministry Associate for Interfaith Work. "The basic fact is that Christianity as it was born in the mind of this Jewish teacher and thinker appears as a technique of survival for the oppressed . . . 'In him was life; and the life was the light of men.' Wherever his spirit appears, the oppressed gather fresh courage; for he announced the good news that fear, hypocrisy, and hatred, the three hounds of hell that track the trail of the disinherited, need have no dominion over them."[16]

The Shepherd, as well.

An Invitation to Faith

Jan and I came over here to Boston four years ago in order to invest the last quarter of our ministry in the next generation of preachers, teachers, ministers of the gospel. You hear today six voices that will change the world for the better. I asked them, in Thurmanesque fashion, to tell me about their sense of the divine, about presence, about shepherd. Here is what they said:

14. Thurman, *Jesus and the Disinherited*, 88.
15. Thurman, *Jesus and the Disinherited*, 53.
16. Thurman, *Jesus and the Disinherited*, 29.

Jesus
is all the world to me . . .
loves me . . .
is perpetually ripe . . .
means freedom . . .
shows us that self-giving love is the way to life [John] . . .
is my transforming friend . . .
has got my back . . .
is the consoler of the poor . . . the lamp of the poor . . .
is unconditional love . . .
is the constant companion on life's journey . . .
My greatest gift . . .
Patient pursuer . . .
In love with us . . .
the Hound of Heaven . . .
Friend on the Journey . . .
challenges us because he loves us . . .
brings out our best self . . .

Now, we ask you, as we sing the hymns of Easter: How will you live out the deep river truths, presence and shepherd? How will you live down its opposition, however you understand it? Have you truly intuited the brevity of life? Have you really absorbed the capacity we have as humans to harm others? Have you faced the dualism of decision that is the marrow of every Sunday, every prayer, every sermon, every service? Are you ready to make a break for it? Are you ready to discover freedom in disappointment and grace in dislocation? Are you set to place one hand in that of The Presence, and the other in that of The Shepherd?

Katherine Kennedy, the director of Boston University's Howard Thurman Center for Common Ground, once said, "The beauty of Thurman is that he wasn't trying to convert people to Christianity. Rather, he wanted people to see that there is a common ground we can reach by respecting one another's differences, while still holding onto those beliefs that are uniquely ours."[17]

As we reflect on such questions, may we do so in the confidence of freedom and grace:

Known in the promise of this season
Reflected in the joys of springtime

---

17. Craig, "Thurman Center Director."

Overheard in the words and vows of commitment
Expanded into the lengthening evening daylight
Enjoyed in the gatherings of families and friends
Celebrated in the ceremonies of completion
And carried forward from this hour of worship and day of remembrance.
In the words of Emily Dickinson:

> I stepped from plank to plank
> So slow and cautiously;
> The stars about my head I felt,
> About my feet the sea.
>
> I knew not but the next
> Would be my final inch—
> This gave me that precarious gait
> Some call experience.[18]

---

18. Dickinson, "Experience," 68.

8

Snow Day

Mark 1:29–39
Delivered at Boston University Marsh Chapel
January 23, 2011

It is perhaps unfortunate that we in the frozen north have not allowed a powerfully central feature of our existence to teach us more about God. We have shoveled snow. We have groveled before storms. We have muffled our pleas for warmth. We have stifled our spouse's prayer, "take me to San Diego." We have trifled with the gruesome details of the weather channel. Shovel, grovel, muffle, stifle, trifle as we may, however, we have not fully considered the gracious presence of snow—and it is high time we did, thank you very much. James Sanders, a teacher of the Older Testament in Rochester and New York City, taught us to first theologize, then moralize. So before in moral indignation we lift another shovel, let us reason together about the gracious presence of snow.

I have only one "Category A" complaint about Boston: there are not enough snow days here. The schools rarely close, and the city rarely stops its commerce. There is a strength in this abstinence from snow days, but there is also a weakness.

Grace Prevenient

On the eastern end of Lake Ontario, whence cometh some wisdom, there is more snow and there are more snow days, in Watertown and Pulaski and Syracuse. Sandy Creek took on fifty-four inches of snow a few weeks ago, that town on Route 11, which we call "a little bit of heaven on Route 11."

That was a snow day, on the Tug Hill Plateau. And a snow day is one day within the day of God on which all our strivings cease. A day that takes from our souls strain and stress and lets our ordered lives confess the beauty of God's peace. A day of preventive interruption, a day of personal reckoning, a day of cleansing health—a day of grace, within the one day of God.

Amazing grace! How sweet the sound . . . of downy flakes . . .

At five o'clock in the morning on a snow day, teachers pray for a day with family. Children implore the ivory goddess to wait upon their needs. Dads look forward to canceling class (though never church), calling in for messages, unbundling the toboggan, digging out that old "tuke," and living, for once, in the interrupted preventive grace of God that says, flake by flake: you are not God.

One of the great anticipated moments of life in our home, a home of teachers and students over some generations, has been the rapt 5 AM televiewing of school closings, for which all fervently pray as in other places people light votive candles or clutch rosary beads or place prayer slips in temple walls. Please, oh please, please let this be a *Snow Day*. A Snow Day is a day of grace.

At judgment day you will not regret having spent a little time away from the office.

Come Sunday, come sundown, you will forget the many ordinary days, but the Snow Day—the day of Dad's chili bean soup, the day of igloos cut with precision, the day of chipping ice from the roof together, the day of grace—this you will take with you into God's presence, as a foretaste of heaven.

God knows, we need prevenient interruption. Otherwise, we think too much of our own doing, and too little of God.

What counts in life is the love of God.

What matters in existence is the grace of God.

What needs doing most, God has already done.

What costs most, God has given.

What we can trust, God has offered.

So, says Saint Paul, we do not preach ourselves—what we might do, what we might be, what we might accomplish—we preach "Jesus Christ, and him crucified."[1] Listen again to 1 Corinthians 11 . . .

If we are not careful, if we do not accept the Snow Day, the day of prevenient grace, then we end up demanding godly things of our spouse, expecting godly achievement of ourselves, requiring godly performance of our church, worshipping the creature and not the Creator, sculpting golden calves, and doing what most humans most of the time do—practicing idolatry.

There is one God, and you are not God, nor is your husband, nor is your pastor, nor is your boss, nor is your parent, nor is your friend. Camus might say, and rightly so, that culture is meant mainly as a setting wherein we remind each other that none of us is God: "On condition that it is understood that they correct one another, and that a limit, under the sun, shall curb them all. Each tells the other that he is not God."[2] Says Dorothy Day to Wall Street: *You are not God.* Says Julian Bond to White America: *You are not God.* Says Betty Friedan to the old boy network: *You are not God.* Says the Republican Congress to the Democratic president: *You are not God.* And what does the president say? And in the new millennium, John Doe will remind women that they are not God either, and Jane Smith will remind children that they are not God either, and, if we can muster a little humility, we will all get by together, singing, *I am not God and you are not God, and we are not God together.*

But it takes a Snow Day, the interrupting, preventing grace of God.

One Snow Day, fifteen years ago, when I was dyingly anxious to finish my PhD, resurrect Methodism, become financially independent, and win Father of the Year awards—all by the close of business that Tuesday, ASAP—I happened to stop, in the late afternoon, for a pastoral call, another important interrupt. An elderly botany professor, known for her guided tours of nature and popular courses at Syracuse University, and once seen in her midseventies swinging from the limb of a sycamore tree that she partly climbed in order to make some now forgotten scholarly point, recited this little charmer to me on a brilliantly snowy day as we drank tea in the later afternoon. Cold it was that day, and snowy, a day for limericks, and laughter and love.

---

1. 1 Cor 2:2, NRSVUE.
2. Camus, *The Rebel* [*L'Homme révolté*], 306.

There once was a parson named Fiddle
Who refused to accept a degree.
   For he said, "'Tis enough
   to be Fiddle,
Without being Fiddle, DD."

She included the poem in a card a few years later, at graduation, to make sure I did not miss the point. Do you get it?

Says the snow to you and me: *fiddledeedee, Fiddle DD*.

Grace Liberative

When Saint Augustine, in the fourth century, was asked to teach his people about the Triune God, he offered this analogy: God the Father is like the sun in the sky that lights and illumines and warms and gives life; God the Son is like the ray of sunlight that carries life and light and illumination and love to us; God the Spirit is like the touch of that sunray upon our cheek, which sustains and helps us, and which personally we feel.[3]

But Augustine in sun and sand, like the young Camus. He preached with an African swing in his rhetoric: *bona bona, dona dona*—good gifts, good gifts.[4] Had Augustine lived in Boston and not along the sunny beaches of North Africa, had he lived in the cold Northern climate and not amid blue sky and ocean view and warmth in February—I mean, hello? What kind of life is that?—had he your perspective on reality, he might rather have offered this analogy: God the Father is like a great cumulonimbus cloud moving over the earth, ready to cover and cleanse and beautify; God the Son is like snow, lovely snow, falling upon us to cover and cleanse and beautify; God the Spirit is like the touch of each unique flake upon our tongues and cheeks as we skate on the Frog Pond and feel personally a power that does cover and cleanse and beautify.

Think how the Scripture would be different if it had come from New England and not the warm climate of Palestine . . .

And God separated the snow banks from the snow banks, those under the firmament from those over the firmament, and God called the firmament heaven. And there was evening and morning, a second day . . .

---

3. Augustine, *Soliloquies*, 537–47.

4. From Latin: *bona* "good," *dona* "gift." In his *De Bono Coniugali* [*On the Good of Marriage*], Augustine outlines three fundamental values, or "goods," of marriage.

And Abraham took his huskies to drink by the frozen lake, and there met Rebekah, who came to break the ice and draw water. And he said, "Pray, put down your pickaxe and let me drink from the icy flow..."

And Pharaoh's daughter saw a sled come by downhill, in which there was wrapped in a snowsuit, a little boy, named Moses. Pharaoh's daughter took him home, and warmed him by the fire...

After the children of Israel had skated across the frozen Blue Sea, and Pharaoh's army was in close pursuit, the Lord God sent a heat wave that melted the ice and Pharaoh, and his chariots and his army plunged down into the briny deep...

By the icicles of Babylon we sat down and wept as our tormentors said to us, sing to us one of the songs of Zion...

Save me, O God! For the avalanche has cascaded upon me... I have fallen into deep drifts and the snow sweeps over me...

Many snow drifts cannot bury love, neither can blizzards smother it...

Let Justice roll down like an avalanche, and righteousness as an unending blizzard...

I baptize you with snow, but one is coming who will baptize you with fire...

Except a man be born of snow and the spirit, he will not enter the kingdom of heaven...

God sends his snow upon the just and the unjust alike...

The wise man built his house upon the rock. The snow fell, and the blizzard came, and the lake effect wind blew and beat upon that house, but it did not fall, because it was built upon the rock...

In the winter of 1966 there fell a tremendous snow. Our little village, eleven hundred feet above sea level on the northern edge of the Allegheny Plateau, received a sudden interruption. Schools closed. Programs were canceled. Trips were postponed. For two weeks, the town just stopped in its tracks. After a while, the supplies of milk and bread were running low. Danehy's market sported bare shelves and empty aisles.

There was a gracious and liberating pause. Looking back, I can see the stresses of that year—all of them resounding around the little Colgate campus—racial attacks by town kids; the first thirteen undergraduate women living in the Colgate Inn; Carson Veache's father, an English teacher, burning draft cards and losing his job for it. Down came the snow, freeing us, freeing us from the role of Almighty God, and liberating our souls for an open future in the one day of God.

That week, someone in Hamilton probably sat by the fire and read Josiah Royce: "The world is the object of an all-inclusive and divine insight, which is thus the supreme reality."[5] Or Unamuno: "*Cuídate sólo de cómo aparezcas ante Dios, cuídate de la idea que de ti Dios tenga.*"[6]

Grace is not something you do, it is something that happens to you. Love is not something you own, it is something you receive and return. And sin is not taking what is offered.

I thought about this again, reading *The Boston Globe* on Thursday. I love to read the *Globe*. I love the occasional stories from the seacoast, about fishing and scrimshaw and seafaring and lighthouses. I also love the long, detailed, personal obituaries, like the one beautifully written for Rev. Wells Grogan, formerly of First Church, Cambridge. There was grace upon grace. "'I have my greatest sense of well-being while flying,' he liked to say."[7] His friends and parishioners remembered his preaching: "When his sermon was about to start, I'd settle in with great anticipation," said one. They remembered his courage: "He showed us how to examine our own selves and be honest, brutally honest," said one. They remembered his pastoral conversation: "He also knew how to have you over to the house and pour a glass of sherry and relax and have informal conversations," said another. But it was the conclusion of the obituary that stood out:

> One [story Grogan told] was about his time as a prisoner of war, when the bread of life was more than metaphorical. "He was elected by the other prisoners to slice the bread; they had a half a loaf for 50 men.... They trusted him to be fair. And when we went to his home, he would slice the bread and tell us the story of when he was a prisoner, when he sliced so evenly that every slice was the same thickness as the others."

When the Ten Commandments proved not enough on their own—true and utterly on point as they are—God came to us, human to human, to free us from idolatry and settle a Snow Day on all our pride.

---

5. Royce, "Office of the Reason," 116.

6. From Spanish: "Think only of how you appear to God, think only of the idea that God has of you." Unamuno, "El sepulcro de don Quijote" ["The Sepulcher of Don Quixote"], 27. English translation from "The Sepulcher of Don Quixote," 97.

7. Quotes in this paragraph from "Rev. Wells Grogan."

Grace Cleansing

Snow interrupts. Snow invades and liberates. Snow falls from on high, heaven sent. Snow falls as friendly presence, freeing its recipients of study, of work, of routine, and allowing, even forcing, a moment of conviviality, and community, and time and space for family and exercise and unexpected pause. Snow is unpredictable, uncontrollable, varied, dangerous, seasonal, cleansing, soothing, quieting and disquieting, cool, comforting, friendly, and free. Snow falls upon us like grace, or grace falls upon us like snow.

Here is a trusting voice, like the one joyfully remembered in *The Boston Globe* this past week.

Our Scripture today, a declaration of grace, puts all this very simply, all this about grace preventive and grace liberative and grace cleansing: he cured many.

This is personal! I had my own first Snow Day Friday!

I wonder about you this week. Will you accept a Snow Day if it is offered? Can you accept the white blanket of grace falling around your shoulders? Could you relax a bit, rely a bit, on the grace of God?

Here:
Would you accept the grace that gave you life?
That is Baptism.

Would you accept the grace that gives you the faith of Jesus Christ?
That is confirmation.

Would you accept the grace that gives you salvation?
That is Holy Communion.

Would you accept the grace that gives you companionship?
That is marriage.

Would you accept the grace that gives you forgiveness?
That is prayer and counsel.

Would you accept the grace that gives you a calling?
That is ordination.

Would you accept the grace that calls you home?
That is blessing, in the extreme and at the last.

So we will recite with Paul,

> It is no longer I who live,
> but it is Christ who lives in me.
> And the life I now live in the flesh
> I live by the faith of the Son of God,
> who loved me and gave himself for me.[8]

---

8. Gal 2:20, NRSVUE.

9

A Rumor of Angels

Mark 10:35–45
Delivered at Boston University Marsh Chapel
Parents Weekend: October 21, 2012

AFTER MY DAD DIED two years ago, we began to go through his things, as families do. Desk, tools, books, guns, clothes (order, play, hope, justice, humor). We did not make much progress at first. We still have not made that much. His desk, somewhat more ordered, is laden drawer after drawer. The many tools, both inherited from earlier generations and purchased as needed over a lifetime, still lie here and there in the basement. A dollhouse, made for a granddaughter and then taken in for repairs years ago, and then left unattended, did migrate to the home of the great-granddaughter. The guns—a relic of another time in the woods, hunting deer in northern New York—were carefully removed by two lawyer siblings. The papers and records now are in boxes with little titles—an improvement of sorts. His clothes still hang in the old closet. I was either assigned, or self-assigned, or asked (or not) to begin to take care of the books: forty year's worth of books in the lifetime library of a Methodist preacher whose preaching teacher at Boston University, Allan Knight Chalmers (for whom I was named), had admonished his pupils to read one book every day. That is to say: there were more than a few books to look through.

I dawdled, lollygagged, procrastinated, avoided, and otherwise shirked my solemn duty. I asked all those I could to go through the library and take at least two books. The books are mostly signed and dated, and of course they have the personal underlining and notes that are typical for most of us. I appropriated a few: a set of Jacques Ellul, for a Lenten series two years ago; a few books from BU faculty—Booth, Chalmers, Bowne; sermon collections from Weatherhead, Gomes, Tittle, Fosdick; others. But I found my progress slow and slower. With each book, my willingness to skim and skip diminished. I found my interest in his notes increasing, and my attention to his underlining expanding. I dream, on and off, of a large oaken door, heavy with metal locks, unopened, chained shut: my dad on one side and I on the other. In the lasting grief I feel at the earthly loss of my dad, it has happened that his preacher's library has become a kind of spiritual bridge, a mode of ongoing conversation between us.

I wonder, this Parents Weekend, given the more limited but still mammoth separation involved in the move to college and the emptying of the home, what healthy conversation, and modes of conversation, may emerge among and between the parents and young adult children here this morning? How will a new mode of conversation emerge, across a new divide, for you? "New occasions teach new duties,"[1] and also sometimes require new forms of conversation, and also, happily, new or different topics and themes in conversation. Let me suggest something. I wonder whether, in these four or three or two years, at least now and then, you—parents and offspring—may find natural, organic ways to think together about religious experience. Let me immediately identify, though, that I mean religious experience that is not so much religious as it is real experience. There is a range of life through which there radiates, like morning sunlight, high and deep and piercingly *real* experience. Most of this range of experience is not, or not only, in worship or liturgy or ecclesiastical involvement or patterned devotion—these are, of course, crucial and important, but more as signposts than as the actual meadows and still waters of religious (that is to say, nonreligious) religious experience.

One day this summer, on one of my less than fruitful forays into the library, I came upon a book, the title of which, *A Rumor of Angels*,[2] is

1. Lowell, "Present Crisis," st. 18.
2. Doubleday, 1969.

borrowed for this morning's sermon. Published in 1969, hardly more than a hundred pages, accessible to clergy and lay alike, brisk and direct in style, sprinkled with salt and light in humor and aphorism, the book, it happens, was written by a Boston University colleague and friend of mine, the premier sociologist of religion of our time, Peter Berger. Professor Berger has graciously endured lunches and conversation, including some semi-successful jokes, with me over these last few years. I knew of this book, both its title and its general argument, which is that God is not dead, religion is not dead, and religious experience is not entirely absent from this earthly vale of tears. But I had never read it. I stuffed the book in my bag.

It is hard to try to recreate the context, 1968, in which Berger was writing and thinking what hardly anyone else was thinking and writing. I will not try to do so. But try to imagine, or remember, a time when *Time* magazine's cover read, "Is God Dead?" Or when the most potent religious word was "secular." Or when administrative malfeasance led to a drug experiment on Good Friday in the basement of Marsh Chapel. Or when the most successful camp meeting was a mud-soaked musical weekend in the Upstate New York village of Woodstock. Just when all hell was breaking loose, Berger wrote about heaven. Like debate participants try to do, he caused people to take a second look at something, or someone.

There is a scene in a Woody Allen movie[3] where, standing in line at a movie theater, Allen's character bickers with another moviegoer about the work of philosopher Marshall McLuhan. Woody Allen crosses the lobby and produces Marshall McLuhan himself! McLuhan proceeds to say, in some fashion, *everything you have just said is totally bogus*. In two weeks, over lunch, I will check with the author himself about my renderings. His book is so lastingly potent because he is writing about all of us, and he is especially writing about you. There is transcendence—he speaks of the "supernatural"—all about us. Maybe that is why you have come, together, to worship on this Parents Weekend. What are the signposts, the clues to transcendence we should look for in our lived experience? Berger's summary still works. You may surprised by the clues he names, the rumors of angels he overhears.

First, give a little credit to your own blessed rage for *order*. Some of you are hoarders, of sorts, and bring order by refusing to get rid of anything. Others are the very opposite: *when in doubt, throw it out*. You have a desire to see things set right, one way or another. What were those kids doing at

---

3. Allen, dir., *Annie Hall*.

Woodstock, in the mud, listening to Janis Joplin, fifty years ago? They were shouting to the heavens that things were not right, that something was out of order. Berger:

> This is the human faith in order as such, a faith closely related to man's fundamental trust in reality. This faith is experienced not only in the history of societies and civilizations, but in the life of each individual—indeed, child psychologists tell us there can be no maturation without the presence of this faith at the outset of the socialization process. Man's propensity for order is grounded in a faith or trust that, ultimately, reality is "in order," "all right," "as it should be."[4]

Do you have a longing for order? Underneath, just there, is a mode of religious experience. Talk a bit about it, parents and children.

Second, and swinging to a different spot, pause and meditate a little on your own enjoyment of *play*. I see grown men enthralled on a green field, following a wee little white ball, which seems to have a mind of its own, for three or four hours in the hot sun. I see grown women shopping together without any particular need, but immersed, self-forgetful, in the process of purchasing God knows what. I see emerging adults fixed and fixated, for days on end, in the *World of Warcraft*. Families were mesmerized this past summer, glued to gymnastics in England. Can you remember playing bridge in college all night long, to the detriment of your zoology grade? Berger: "In playing, one steps out of one time into another. . . . When adults play with genuine joy, they momentarily regain the deathlessness of childhood."[5] (Viewers of the recent film *Moonrise Kingdom*[6] readily understand this.)

> The experience of joyful play is not something that must be sought on some mystical margin of existence. It can readily be found in the reality of ordinary life. . . . The religious justification of the experience can be achieved only in an act of faith . . . This faith is inductive—it does not rest on a mysterious revelation, but rather on what we experience in our common, ordinary lives . . . Under the aspect of inductive faith, religion is the final vindication of childhood and of joy, and of all gestures that replicate these.[7]

4. Berger, *Rumor of Angels*, 67.
5. Berger, *Rumor of Angels*, 72, 73.
6. Anderson, dir., *Moonrise Kingdom*.
7. Berger, *Rumor of Angels*, 75.

One student said: "I played basketball today, on the intramural team—it was awesome." Talk about it a bit, parents and children.

Third, we sense the (my word) supranatural, the transcendent, in the experience of *hope*. Hope does spring eternal in the human breast. Hope keeps us going when otherwise we would not. You may have seen Meryl Streep and Tommy Lee Jones dramatize this in the midst of their struggling marriage in the movie *Hope Springs*. Parents hope their children will thrive in college. Students hope so, too. So do professors and administrators and deans of chapels. We hope. Actually, every autumn, when the suitcases and duffel bags spread out on Bay State Road, I see a tide of hope. It is overwhelmingly beautiful, and tearful given the giving up required by such hope in all directions. (I have not yet spoken, speaking of giving up, of the tuition check payment.) There is something lasting, real, meaningful, costly, and true about hope. Where there is life, there is hope. Better: where there is hope, there is life. People with no regular religion at all know about hope, and its absence. Berger:

> Human existence is always oriented toward the future. Man exists by constantly extending his being into the future, both in his consciousness and in his activity. Put differently, man realizes himself in projects. An essential dimension of this "futurity" of man is hope. It is through hope that men overcome the difficulties of any given here and now. And it is through hope that men find meaning in the face of extreme suffering.
> ... There seems to be a death-refusing hope at the very core of our *humanitas*. While empirical reason indicates that this hope is an illusion, there is something in us that, however shamefacedly in an age of triumphant rationality, goes on saying "no!" and even says "no!" to the ever so plausible explanation of empirical reason ... [Inductive faith] takes into account the intentions within our "natural experience" of hope that point toward a "supernatural" fulfillment.[8]

I wonder if the generations sitting together in the pews this morning might, come Christmas, talk a bit about that most unreligious religious experience: a thing called hope, a place called hope, a time called hope, a feeling called hope. Talk about it a bit, parents and children.

Fourth, we have burning desire to see real *justice* done, and also to see massive injustice called to account. Berger uses, well, the word damnation. I am using slightly different language because I cannot make his argument

---

8. Berger, *Rumor of Angels*, 76, 80.

as well with this word this morning. It is too loaded. But the heart of the intention is true and strong. We want people who get away with murder not, ultimately, to get away with murder. Emil Brunner, after WWII, was asked why he spoke about the devil. He gave two reasons. In sum: *Jesus did. And, I have seen him.* When we think of mass murder, of horrific injustice, intentionally and painstakingly executed, we demand justice. There is something down deep in the human heart that just will not let things go. This is not about forgiveness. It is about retributive justice. Sometimes young people have a keener sense of this than their elders. Berger:

> This refers to experiences in which our sense of what is humanly permissible is so fundamentally outraged that the only adequate response to the offense as well as to the offender seems to be a curse of supernatural dimensions . . .
>
> . . . There are certain deeds that cry out to heaven . . . Not only are we constrained to condemn, and to condemn absolutely, but, if we should be in a position to do so, we would feel constrained to take action on the basis of this certainty. . . .
>
> . . . Deeds that cry out to heaven also cry out for hell. . . . No human punishment is "enough" in the case of deeds as monstrous as these. . . . [This is] a moral order that transcends the human community, and thus invokes a retribution that is more than human.[9]

When adults talk as adults, younger with older, there arise memories and understandings, dark in hue and deep in sentiment, that call out for an extraordinary, unearthly, transcendent justice. How shall we talk about these? Talk a bit, bit by bit, in the years to come, parents and children.

Fifth, one can sense the horizon of heaven, the transcendent radiance of mystery, the supranatural or supernatural, in the simple experience of *humor*, perhaps the very polar opposite of the cry for retributive justice. Here I will pause to tell an ostensibly humorous story. I was asked to pray at the start of a billion-dollar campaign. My reply: "It would be my pressure— I mean, my pleasure."

People ask about interreligious life on campus and I say: "The Hindus are the most Christian people I deal with." Phyllis Diller died this year. You remember her husband, Fang.[10] You remember her mother-in-law, Moby

---

9. Berger, *Rumor of Angels*, 81, 82-83, 84.

10. Comedian Phyllis Diller invented a fictional husband (named Fang), mother-in-law (Moby Dick), and sister-in-law (Captain Bligh), to whom she often referred in her comedy routines.

Dick. You remember her sister-in-law, Captain Bligh. You remember her self-deprecation: "I once wore a peekaboo blouse. People would peek and then they'd boo." You remember her cackling laughter. Humor, real humor, stops time still. "He who sits in the heavens laughs,"[11] says the psalmist. Berger:

> There is one fundamental discrepancy from which all other comic discrepancies are derived—the discrepancy between man and universe.... *The comic reflects the imprisonment of the human spirit in the world.*...
>
> Humor mocks the "serious" business of this world and the mighty who carry it out... Power is the final illusion, while laughter reveals the final truth....
>
> ... It is Quixote's hope rather than Sancho Panza's "realism" that is ultimately vindicated, and the gestures of the clown have a sacramental dignity.[12]

When you gather at Thanksgiving table, after the prayer and before the turkey, tell one funny story, or one joke, or one humorous memory. Talk a bit, talk a bit, talk a bit, parents and children.

Here is our theme. Order, play, hope, justice, humor: religious experiences without recourse to religion. You may not be so religious, or so you think. But do you create order, and crave play, and desire hope, and long for justice, and enjoy humor? These are signs, for you—signs of something else, something lasting and true and good and extraordinary. Talk a bit about it, parents and children. As Bonnie Raitt put it: "Let's give 'em something to talk about!"

For our gospel today, from Mark 10, accosts us in this very way. "Are you able to drink the cup that I drink...?"[13] asks Jesus. "Whoever wishes to become great among you must be your servant, and whoever wishes to be first among you must be slave of all. For the Son of Man came not to be served but to serve and to give his life a ransom for many."[14]

Parents, students, community, listeners: can you drink that cup?

Sursum Corda: things are not quite always as they seem, says the gospel. There is more than a little difference between appearance and reality, says the gospel. Real leaders serve others, says the gospel. Ambition unfettered

---

11. Ps 2:4, NRSVUE.
12. Berger, *Rumor of Angels,* 87, 88-89, 90. (Italics in the original.)
13. Mark 10:38, NRSVUE.
14. Mark 10:43-45, NRSVUE.

will not lead to happiness, says the gospel. A true life is not always an easy one, says the gospel. The Son of man did not come to be served, but to serve, says the gospel. There is a mystery at the heart of life, says the gospel, and that mystery is "Jesus Christ and him crucified,"[15] one whose life, true life, is poured out like a ransom paid to free others. Underneath the tiny things lurk the great things. A mystery, a ransom paid, a life laid up and laid out and laid down, lurking, waiting, present, like a breath, the eternal great things hidden under the unlikely blankets of the littlest things. Your calling to faith may be brewing . . . under a desire for order. Under a love of play. Under a feeling of hope. Under a longing for justice. Under a sense of humor. And all through the cacophony of a noisy world, a hint, a glimmer, an echo, a breath, a rumor . . . of angels.

---

15. 1 Cor 2:2, NRSVUE.

10

Exit or Voice?

Matthew 4:1–11
Romans 5:12–19
Genesis 2:15–17, 3: 1–7
Philippians 1:19–30
Delivered at Boston University Marsh Chapel
March 9, 2014

Scripture

OVER PASTA LAST SUMMER, a hot July night, six of us of long friendship ate and talked. Our dear friend Anita has for decades been a committed lay reader in her summer church. She has taken pride in her work, praying and practicing for her lector role, recruiting others, and helping in worship. With spaghetti and wine, and the warmth of long relationship, we nodded and supped. But something had happened. The old pastor had left. A new one had come. He was, sadly, rude and belligerent with his helpers. Not just once, or twice.

Said Anita: "What should I do? I love to read, and I love my lector team. But his behavior I cannot abide. I have talked to him. He rebuffs me. If I stay, I endure and even collude in his misbehavior, but I will still have my voice in church and with the committee. If I leave, I exit from what I love and also leave behind any influence I might have to help, support, or protect others. I am loyal to my church, but I am ready to go. What should I do?"

Hours, days, and months are actually shot through with this form of dilemma in choice. Exit or stay? A famous study forty years ago laid out for economists the dimensions of the dilemma.[1] But such a condition goes well beyond the marketplace.

Exit is as old the exit from the Garden of Eden. Voice is as old as the dominical voice of Christ resisting temptation. Exit and voice: how do the Scriptures frame such living choice?

Our lessons from Holy Scripture this morning propound the moral and mortal limits of life in sin and death. As does every Sunday benediction, sung or spoken, Genesis 2 and Romans 5 and Matthew 4 directly remind you: your life is brief and messy.

The ancient myth, beginning in the garden of paradise and moving to the east of Eden, entwines fragility and fragmentation, existence and estrangement, sin and death. The tree of the knowledge of good and evil provides the symbolic substance; the serpent provides the symbolic occasion; and the fig leaves provide the symbolic covering of the entanglement of sin and death, shame and loss. The strange world of the Bible—not strange in the sense of odd or wrong, but strange in the sense of numinous and monumental—accosts us today with a ringing reminder of suffering and death.

Others may put these verses in different frames: a pan-religious frame (Joseph Campbell), or a salvation-history frame (Gerhard von Rad), or a tradition-history frame (Rudolf Bultmann), or a literary-religious frame (Diana Eck). For us in worship, though, these words are holy writ. They function as words with divine import for human living. They remind us of moral and mortal limits to life in sin and death, suffering and death. They set before us the perilous multiple choices of life in a certain realistic context, as we shall see in a moment with regard to the choices, hourly and daily, between exit and voice.

The deep, hard cold of a real old-time religion winter season, like ours here in 2014, befits our Holy Scriptures today. It is bracing to feel the full wind and cold of winter. We are thus reminded, perhaps even made mellow and melancholy—no bad thing—by the stern, icy reminder of morality and mortality, sin and death.

This Lent, we engage as our conversation partner the great Geneva Protestant Reformer John Calvin (1509-64). We have found it helpful,

---

1. Hirschman, *Exit, Voice, and Loyalty*, 1970.

in this season, to link our preaching here at Marsh Chapel, a historically Methodist pulpit, with voices from the related but distinct Reformed tradition, which has been so important in New England over four hundred years. The Methodist tradition has emphasized human freedom; the Reformed, divine freedom. During Lent each year,[2] we have brought the two into some interaction both harmonious and dissonant. It is fitting that we begin with Genesis 2. Genesis 1 is a more Anglican chapter, if you will, representing the goodness of creation. Genesis 2 and 3 are more Calvinist, if you will, representing the fallen character of creation, known daily to us in sin, death, and the threat of meaninglessness. Both traditions, English and French, make space for both creation and fall. But the emphasis is different: one more garden, the other more serpent; one more creation, the other more fall.

Our passage from Romans 5 gives us Paul's own apocalyptic rendering of the themes of sin and death. We should be careful to recognize that the words are the same here as in Genesis 2 and 3, but the meanings are different. For Paul, both sin and death are spheres of influence, orbs of control, dominions and principalities and powers. His apocalyptic worldview makes a changed use of the inherited terms from Genesis. Likewise, his philosophical mode is quite different from the narrative structures in Genesis 2 and 3. The freedom found in Christ smashes the controls of the orbs of sin and death, for Paul.

So Calvin writes, about this passage: "*To sin*, is to be corrupt and faulty. For that natural [de]pravity which we bring out of our mother's womb, although it do not so soon show forth his fruits, yet, nevertheless, it is sin before the Lord, and deserveth his vengeance . . . Grace signifieth the mere goodness of God, or his free love, whereof he gave a testimony in Christ, that he might help our misery."[3] You did hear the Apostle say that this grace was given to all men. That sounds fairly universalistic to most readers. *All*. Yet Calvin says otherwise: Paul "maketh it a grace common to all, because it is offered to all. Not that all men are partakers of it indeed; for albeit Christ suffered for the sins of the whole world, and he indifferently, through the goodness of God offered unto all, yet all do not receive him."[4]

2. Calvin represents the chief resource for other Lenten conversation partners we at Marsh Chapel have engaged in the past, such as Marilynne Robinson (2013), Jacques Ellul (2012), Dietrich Bonhoeffer (a Lutheran cousin)(2011), and other themes we have discussed in the past, like "Atonement" (2009) and "Decision" (2008).

3. Calvin, *Commentary*, 135, 140. (Italics in the original.)

4. Calvin, *Commentary*, 143.

Like that wind you felt on the Esplanade the other day, these sentences, from Geneva in 1540 or so, have their purposes. They posit that we are not in possession of grace as much as we are in need of grace. Grace is the gift of God sorely needed by the people of God. One hundred thirty thousand dead in Syria. A four-year-old pummeled to death in New England. A mother in Daytona Beach driving into the surf with her children. Construct your own list, following a good reading of the Sunday newspaper. A cold, sober realism is found both in Romans 5, on Calvin's reading, and in the daily reports of suffering, near and far.

Our passage from Matthew 4 connects with Adam and Christ along the trail of temptation from the garden of Eden to the wilderness of Palestine. This Gospel, a teacher's gospel, makes sure to begin with the harder news: that even Christ himself was tempted to make improper use of freedom. In Calvin's view, every form of temptation comes with a divine purpose, a gracious protection, and a form of grace to be received. "We should realize that the temptations that strike us are not fortuitous, or the turn of Satan's whim, without God's permission, but that the Spirit of God presides in all our trials, that our faith may be the better tried. So we may take sure hope, that God, who is the supreme Master of the ring, will not be unmindful of us, or fail to succor our weaknesses, as He sees we are unequal to them."[5]

In January, William Faulkner's *Go Down, Moses* stood out from others on a bookstore shelf. A sort of novel, it is, as powerful as it is impenetrable: "Himself his own battleground, the scene of his own vanquishment and the mausoleum of his defeat. . . . There is only one thing worse than not being alive, and that's shame. . . . They can learn nothing save through suffering, remember nothing save when underlined in blood."[6]

Experience

How shall we use our human freedom faithfully in the light of the divine freedom known to us in Christ?

Exit or voice or resignation? Fight or flight or play dead?

Your roommate smokes for breakfast, drugs for lunch, drinks for dinner. Do you leave—him, school, or both? Do you confront—"One of us is crazy, and I think it's you?" Do you grin and bear it?

---

5. Calvin, *Harmony of the Gospels*, 135-36.
6. Faulkner, *Go Down, Moses*, 168, 186, 286.

Your faculty has taken a new direction—that is, a wrong turn. For well-intentioned reasons, they have exchanged birthright for pottage. Do you politick, agitate, criticize, and combat in what may well be a losing cause? Do you call a friend who has long wanted to hire you at Brown or NYU, and prepare to exit? Or do you close your door, grade your papers, and play a little more golf?

Your brother is about to marry the wrong woman. He is impressionable, and she is impressive—an empress, if you will. Do you shout a warning and risk never speaking to him again? Do you reason, consult, have lunch, empathize, and appeal to the better angels of his nature? Do you throw up your hands, send an early shower gift, and bite your tongue?

You are a major world superpower. With limited success, you have partially pacified a resentful Middle Eastern nation. Now what? Do you exit stage left, leaving behind a decade of warfare, tens of thousands dead, tribal hatreds still much in evidence, and hope for the best? Do you stay, increase your footprint and military presence, give voice to the rights and needs of children, women, religious minorities, and others? Or do you practice a little benign neglect, and put your energy into health care, immigration reform, nuclear disarmament, Chinese economics, and the next election?

How much for exit and how much for voice? How much for flight and how much for fight? And, then, when do you just pull your turtle head back into your shell and play dead?

In AD 54, Paul of Tarsus, the Apostle to the Gentiles, in a verse with subterranean links to Genesis and Matthew, exit and voice, wrestled with the same angel-demon.

On one hand, he wrote, "For to me, living is Christ and dying is gain . . . I cannot say which I will choose."[7] For once his regular apocalyptic eschatology, the horizontal primitive hope of the day of the Lord, which he fully expects to see in the flesh, gives way to a simple, vertical, Greek, gnostic eschatology, an immediate translation to glory. Troubles—trouble in the churches, it may be—spark Paul's momentary exit strategy, his longing to "depart and be with Christ."[8]

On the other hand, he considered, "to remain in the flesh is more necessary for you."[9] *I am for you, so I should be with you. It is better for you that I am here.* We can add: to raise my voice, to lift my voice, to write my letters,

---

7. Phil 1:21-22, NRSVUE.
8. Phil 1:23, NRSVUE.
9. Phil 1:24, NRSVUE.

to preach my gospel, to have influence into the next generation. Paul longs for exit. Paul lives for voice.

How much for exit? How much for voice? How much Protestant exit? How much Catholic loyalty? How much Reformation? How much Counter-Reformation? How much pulpit? How much table? How much discontinuity? How much continuity? How much new world? How much old world?

On these spiritual balances hang the cure of our souls. Needless to say, there is not an answer, no formulaic response, no "one size fits all," no ethical Procrustean bed. Another Pauline verse beckons: "Let all be fully convinced in their own minds."[10] We could, in faith, though, at least carry away from Lent 1 some shared understandings as people of faith.

We understand that on a daily (if not hourly) basis, we are choosing, by the freedom of the will, between exit and voice. To have voice means to have to stay. To exit means to give up voice. To exit may be your statement, your voice, within a certain context, but it is, then, your valediction, your swan song. On the other hand, your voice may be your exit, but it is then a prophetic utterance, with all the continuing costs attested in the four greater and twelve lesser prophecies of our Hebrew scripture. Or you could just sit this one out, take a siesta.

We understand that most decisions involve some admixture, some balance—neither Webster only nor Calhoun only, but the shadow of Henry Clay, the great compromiser.

We understand that where we place our physical self, our body, where we place our standard on the field of battle, our social location, makes a difference. Starting with showing up for worship, to speak with our neighbors, to sing the hymns of faith, to utter our prayers, to attend to the Word.

We understand, too, that whatever voice we lift, even the muted voice of silent witness, has a hearing, makes a difference, marks our faith, and influences the faith of others.

Exit? Voice?

Over forty years, in painful relationship to my beloved Methodist Church, I along with others have struggled about exit and voice. Many of my friends, colleagues, students, and companions have chosen exit, one way or another. In some limited ways, I have, too. These are faithful people making hard decisions. I honor the cradle Methodist who chooses

---

10. Rom 14:5, NRSVUE.

Episcopal orders, the Methodist seminarian who reluctantly becomes a Congregationalist, the Gen X and millennial cohorts leaving us behind.

I stay. I stay to raise my voice, and to reject giving my orders, my position, my influence, and, over time, multiple generations of pastoral leadership, to a currently Afrocentric general church. I stay because I believe that over time, around the world, under the influence of a self-correcting spirit of truth loose in the universe, the mighty scourge of homophobia will be rejected by a body that in its singing voice and reasonable mind—in its spiritual bones—lives the gospel of freedom, grace, love, acceptance, kindness, and forgiveness. Over time, Methodists will not want to harm nine-year-old gay children.

But. This response is *generational*. It will take longer than my limited lifetime for this change fully to come. This response is *global*. It will require a change of heart, over time, in African Methodists. This response is *gritty*. It will mean underground railways to marry gays and deploy ordained gays. It will mean prayer and withholding apportionment dollars. It will mean seasoned, *genuine* response in many settings: charge, annual, jurisdictional, global, and intergalactic conferences. It will mean *hupomone*—long-suffering, long-suffering, long-suffering. It will involve political love.

(Political love—active love in institutional life—is a crucial, necessary feature of realistic faithfulness. Political love is political because it occurs by intention within the city community. Political love is love because it is divinely gracious—an incursive addition to life.

Love listens and remembers. Love compliments with sincerity and pointed limitation. Love watches for another's unspoken longing. Love uncovers festering injustice. Love shows up, attends, responds, and then invites.

This political love accepts the requirement of alliance, even alliance with opposition, without neglecting friendships, or forgetting the beauty of friendship.)

Dag Hammarskjöld: "God does not die on the day when we cease to believe in a personal deity, but we die on the day when our lives cease to be illumined by the steady radiance, renewed daily, of a wonder, the source of which is beyond all reason."[11]

Exit or voice? You be the judge.

---

11. Hammarskjöld, *Markings*, 56.

11

Sweet Chariot

2 Kings 2:1–12
John 2:13–22
Delivered at Boston University Marsh Chapel
March 8, 2015

IN (OR NEAR) THE year 850 BCE, the prophet Elijah stood against the prophets of Baal on Mount Carmel. He alone stood against four hundred and fifty. The enemy prophets called on Baal to bring fire. Baal did not. But Yahweh did, at Elijah's imprecation. "Cry aloud! Surely he is a god; either he is meditating, or he has wandered away, or he is on a journey, or perhaps he is asleep and must be awakened."[1] *Maybe he does not hear well. Try again.* Elijah also announced the end of a great drought. This was on the way to the river Jordan.

In the year 820 BCE, Elijah went up a high mountain, not unlike that on which Jesus stood some weeks ago in the Gospel of Mark, and listened for God. He heard God. Not in fire, or smoke, or whirlwind, or techno-wizardry, or techno-frenzy. For God was not there. But in a still small voice. In silence, the silence before hearing and speech. In conscience. In mind

---

1. 1 Kgs 18:27, NRSVUE.

and will. "The Lord passed by, and a great and strong wind rent the mountains and brake in pieces the rocks before the Lord; but the Lord was not in the wind: and after the wind an earthquake; but the Lord was not in the earthquake: and after the earthquake a fire; but the Lord was not in the fire: and after the fire a still small voice."[2] On the way to the river Jordan.

In the year 800 BCE, Elijah, the troubler of Israel, saw King Ahab, through his wife Jezebel, take the garden of a poor man, Naboth, and kill Naboth in the process. "I will give you a better vineyard for it,"[3] said Ahab. But Naboth did not want another. And "Ahab went home resentful and sullen . . . He lay down on his bed, turned away his face, and would not eat."[4] But Naboth held on to his vineyard. "His wife Jezebel said to him, 'Do you now govern Israel? Get up, eat some food, and be cheerful; I will get you the vineyard of Naboth the Jezreelite.'"[5] But Naboth resisted her, too. "So they took him outside the city and stoned him to death . . . Jezebel said to Ahab, 'Go, take possession of the vineyard of Naboth the Jezreelite, which he refused to give you for money, for Naboth is not alive but dead.'"[6] But Elijah confronted the king. "Have you killed and also taken possession? . . . In the place where dogs licked up the blood of Naboth, dogs will also lick up your blood."[7] Elijah, the troubler of Israel. It is one thing to desire another's property, and another to take it by force. Elijah held a mirror before the country that wanted such a king and the influence of such a queen. On the way to the river Jordan.

In the year AD 30, Elijah's spirit awakened Peter, who went with Jesus up a high mountain to see him changed. Elijah brought reason and morality to the religion Moses founded. Lent is meant to remind us of the priority of worship. Find a way to get to worship. Worship brings the insight of personal need, lifted in prayer. Worship brings the insight of another's hurt, lifted in communal, singing, four-part harmonic hymns. Worship brings the insight of clarity, a word fitly spoken, lifted in the sermon. Worship brings the insight of choosing, the choice of faith, not thrill but will, lifted in the invitations to devotion, discipline, dedication. Worship brings the insight of loyalty, of heart, lifted every Sunday in the offering of gifts and

2. 1 Kgs 19:11-12, KJV.
3. 1 Kgs 21:2, NRSVUE.
4. 1 Kgs 21:4, NRSVUE.
5. 1 Kgs 21:7, NRSVUE.
6. 1 Kgs 21:13-15, NRSVUE.
7. 1 Kgs 21:19, NRSVUE.

tithes. Elijah brought hope, prophetic hope, into the tradition and minds of his people. On the way from the river Jordan.

In the year 1735, the spirit of Elijah rested on the New England community of North Hampton, and the ministry of a Puritan divine, Jonathan Edwards, our Calvinist interlocutor this Lent. Edwards saw the divine light shining in the human soul. Edwards saw that the material universe exists in God's mind. Edwards saw faith in the willingness of saints to be damned for the glory of God. Edwards saw religious affections, inclinations, dispositions, all gifts of God in faith, the love of God that kindles joy, hope, trust, peace, and "a sense of the heart."[8] Edwards saw the centrality of the experience of faith: a person may know that honey is sweet, but no one can know what sweet means until they taste the honey. Edwards saw that God delights properly in the devotions, graces, and good works of his saints. Jonathan "Elijah" Edwards, our New England precursor, walked along the Connecticut River, on the way from the river Jordan.

In the year 1865, in our nation's capital, the spirit of Elijah touched the tongue of Abraham Lincoln. Months and days before Lincoln died, Lincoln cried out, "With malice toward none; with charity for all; with firmness in the right, as God gives us to see the right—let us finish the work we are in."[9] Real cost, real costs, occasion our very freedom to gather in community for worship this morning. The same spirit from 850 BCE, that presence, that quickened consciousness, that affection, that devotion, that inclination was present with Lincoln, and is with us today. You have the brute fact of the brute creation. You have, too, the spirit.

In the year 1951, the spirit of Elijah rested in the mind of Ray Bradbury. He wrote a book, *Fahrenheit 451* (this is the temperature at which paper burns), an eschatological prophecy about the end of books, the end of reading, the end of memory. The novel ends along a river. Guy Montag finds himself with hoboes around a campfire, along the river bank. He is surprised to find that fire, the mode of book destruction he has resisted, can "give as well as take,"[10] warm as well as burn. He waits in the shadows. The men around the fire summon him out of the dark, and take him in. He

---

8. For Edwards's discussions of the sense of the heart, see, for example: *Nature of True Virtue* (Ann Arbor, 1970), *Religious Affections* (New Haven, 1959), and *Philosophy of Jonathan Edwards from his Private Notebooks*, ([Eugene, OR, 1955]). See also: William Wainwright, "Jonathan Edwards and the Sense of the Heart," *Faith and Philosophy: Journal of the Society of Christian Philosophers* 7, no. 1 (1990): article 3.

9. Lincoln, *Speeches*, 361.

10. Bradbury, *Fahrenheit 451*, 133.

learns that each one of them has committed some book to memory. One is living Plato's *Republic*. Others have memorized works by Aristophanes, Confucius, Jefferson, and Lincoln. Byron, Machiavelli, Tom Paine, and the Gospels—Matthew, Mark, Luke, and John—all these are carried in the minds of hoboes, walking libraries, the remaining memory of the art of the race. "What have you to offer?" they ask Montag.[11] Parts of Ecclesiastes and of the Revelation, he replies. In 2015, an age that has eschewed reading for scanning, books for blogs, Google for memory, and earning for knowing, "Elijah" Bradbury's word resonates. On the way out from the river Jordan.

In the year 1959, down in the southern third of Alabama, the spirit of Elijah rested on the mind of Harper Lee. She wrote a book, a great book, a book great because it changed peoples' minds and hearts. Like Augustine's *Confessions*. Like *Uncle Tom's Cabin*. Like *The Diary of Anne Frank*. Like Elie Wiesel's *Night*. Like what Tom Hanks tried to do with *Philadelphia*. The prophet's magic mantel, which divides the river Jordan, pierces the heart. Lee's pastor, our friend Thomas Lane Butts, spoke of her to me some years ago. All on the way from the river Jordan.

In the year 1965, in early March, the spirit of Elijah walked across the Edmund Pettus Bridge in Selma, Alabama. John Lewis was there, not angry, but with "a sense of righteous indignation,"[12] as he said. Through the history, offices, and gifts of Boston University, we sat next to him over dinner three years ago. He wanted to be a preacher, growing up: *I would come home and preach to the chickens*, he remembered. If nothing else, perhaps fifty years hence we could remember that real change is real hard but comes in real time when people really work at it, on the ground, in personal conversation, then in small groups, with gifted leadership. Down on the way from the river Jordan.

In the winter of the year 2015, Elijah, the spirit of Elijah, brooded over the face of New England snow fields. The sore muscles of a shoveling people, the tired torsos of a commuting community, the undaunted willingness still to help a neighbor, the gritty determination to get through the blizzard, the awareness of need for investment in communal forms of transport, the gladness of children and the extra time of adults, the same spirit visited. But also: the sore muscles of memory wrestling with the horror and mayhem—needless and cruel—of Marathon 2013. The blizzard of feeling and thought inevitably brought to the surface by the current courtroom

---

11. Bradbury, *Fahrenheit 451*, 137.
12. Lewis, "Interview with John Lewis," November 6, 1985.

trial. The rush of anger alongside the search for the better angels of one's nature. You may not daily recognize Elijah. But he is present. Morning in reading. Mealtime in prayer. Evening in quiet. Sunday in worship. (People have such odd reasons for avoiding worship.) On the way forward from the river Jordan. Elijah: elusive spirit, mysterious ghost, the divine present absence, personified.

On March 8 of 2015, the spirit of prophet Elijah hovered in the nave of Marsh Chapel, Boston University. The chapel has given, to you and others, over many decades—beauty, grace, preachment, music, recollection. Some here have found God, and some here have been found by God. Marsh Chapel—a gift. And so you have responded. By listening on the radio—good. By joining us one Sunday—good. By giving to, and through, this ministry—good. By inviting someone to listen, too. By inviting someone to come with you. Good. By dreaming of an even more permanent place, and even stronger witness, and even more vibrant voice at Marsh Chapel. One of you may choose to endow the deanship of this chapel. Good. Elijah awaits us. On the way from the river Jordan.

In the year 20??—I apologize, I have mislaid the exact date—the prophet Elijah will be on my doorstep, and knocking on your door. Perhaps at midnight. Maybe at noonday. Possibly at dawn. Or in the wee hours of the morning. The eschatological prophet, the prophet of the last things, the one invited by Peter to a booth with Jesus: Elijah, the prophet of God, will make a pastoral visit. In the last hour of my life, and yours. There will be the river Jordan. There will be a mantel slapped on the water. There will be a parting of the ways. There will be a step forward. There will be a chariot, a sweet chariot, a swinging sweet chariot—a fiery, swinging, sweet chariot. There will be a presence. Could it be that the weeks of cascade, the days of nevada, the snow and snow and snow of our 2015 New England winter of discontent should carry an evocation, a query, a reminder, a call, premonition, a measuring, a warning, a promise? Most of what we spend our time on, and our money, doesn't matter at all. It is the spirit that giveth life.[13]

In the year to come, sometime (going back a half step), an Elijah spirit will usher us toward the book of Harper Lee, a surprise and an adventure. In this newly discovered book,[14] I understand, Scout is grown up, and Atticus Finch is old, and the setting is not the depression but the early civil rights

---

13. A reference to 2 Cor 3:6, KJV.
14. Harper Lee's novel *Go Set a Watchhman* (HarperCollins, 2015) was discovered and published decades after it was written.

movement. We know whence Scout emerged. Maybe we will reread *Mockingbird*. One of my predecessors in Rochester, Andrew Turnipseed, was a southerner, a friend of Dr. King's. At Turnipseed's funeral, T. L. Butts preached:

> Near the end of Nelle Harper Lee's wonderful novel, *To Kill a Mockingbird*, there is a touching and unforgettable scene. Jean Louise (Scout), young daughter of the courageous Atticus Finch, has persuaded her father to let her come to the courtroom to hear the verdict in the controversial case in which he is defending a Black man. She chose to sit in the balcony with the Black people. The inevitable "guilty" verdict is rendered. It is over. Atticus Finch gathers his papers, places them in his briefcase, and begins a sad and lonely walk down the center aisle to the back door. Scout hears someone call her name. "Miss Jean Louise?" She looks behind her and sees that all of the Black people are standing up as her father walks down the aisle. Then she heard the voice of the black minister, Rev. Sykes: "Miss Jean Louise, stand up, stand up, your father's passin'." Can you hear that? It begs to be heard.[15]

Here is one way to live. Elijah's way. The spirit way. The way of confidence born of obedience. The way of the journey of faith, the obedience of faith. In this way, we live with the trust to see things through. To cross over. To cross the river. To trust our past. To trust our experience. To trust the spirit. To trust our Elishas,[16] our friends and successors. To trust that, in some way spiritually similar to Elijah at Jordan, a sweet chariot awaits.

A chariot of promise. A chariot of freedom. A chariot of hope. A chariot of deliverance. A chariot of salvation. A chariot of heaven. A chariot to carry us home.

---

15. Oration by Thomas Lane Butts, 2002. From the author's memory.
16. Elisha is a biblical figure who was a prophet and successor to Elijah.

12

Remembering Elie Wiesel

Matthew 18:21–35
Delivered at Boston University Marsh Chapel
September 17, 2017: Alumni Sunday

Bildungsroman

AFTER SOME SIGNIFICANT INTERNAL struggle, come senior year of college, I finally decided to go to seminary.

That spring, I visited Harvard, Yale, Boston University, and Union Theological Seminary. I stood outside the chapel here, and have a picture to prove it. Union, in New York, was easily the right place for me. In part I went on the advice of a friend that "a year of seminary never hurt anyone." Once in for a penny, I was in for a pound, and really never looked back. Your calling is what you sense is your best response to God. And that can change. In fact, you need to practice the art of editing your dreams.[1] They need writing, but they need editing, too.

What a world opened up at Union in New York City! How grateful I am. The urban world, the ecumenical world, the theological world, the biblical world, the world of the gospel and its preachment. It is an embarrassment to admit to you how little I knew about the Bible, for all my parsonage

---

1. "Don't be afraid to edit your dreams and rewrite the story of what you want to do in life." Tassler, "Commencement Address," May 15, 2016.

tenure, my small Methodist college degree, summer camp leadership, and generational background. I knew nada. And into that mental wasteland vacuum swept Samuel Terrien, George Landes, Raymond Brown, and Lou Martyn, four horsemen of the apocalypse, to furnish its empty mental apartment bookshelves with, well, books. I fell in love with the Bible, with the strange world of the Bible. There too were James Forbes, Cornel West, Christopher Morse, Linda Clark (who later came here), Horace Allen (who came here later), and many others. William Sloane Coffin came into the Riverside pulpit. Across the street was the Jewish Theological Seminary, whence Abraham Heschel had come just a few years earlier to walk around Grant's Tomb with Reinhold Niebuhr in the autumn afternoons. That image of interreligious, interfaith theological discourse inspires still.

It happened that Union was in the throes of a renaissance of sorts, and the president, Donald Shriver Jr., had somehow convinced Robert McAfee Brown—a Union alumnus, longtime faculty member, and Union family member, if you will—to leave his beloved California haunts and come back to New York with his wife Sydney (a missionary's daughter). Bob and Sydney met in the summer home of Reinhold Niebuhr near Heath, Massachusetts—they were, in that sense, godchildren of the Niebuhrs and so of that tradition at Union. Brown stayed at Union only three years, but they were the very three I was there. He had been the Protestant observer at Vatican II and taught a course titled "The Ecumenical Revolution," to which we fought to gain entrance. He knew very well about Heschel and Niebuhr walking in the autumn light on Riverside Drive, because he fell in love and got married under Niebuhr's roof. Brown encouraged us, in 1978, to go and work at the World Council of Churches in Switzerland, in the Office of Urban Ministry run by the one and only George Todd, Brown's fellow Presbyterian.

Due to health issues, we left Union and New York suddenly and precipitously in February of 1979. In that early winter of 1979, we retreated to a church in Ithaca, to heal and to begin the work of ministry among the students at "godless" Cornell. Before we left—perhaps a week or so before—Bob and Sydney Brown held a winter dinner party in their home, which was an apartment in McGiffert Hall, under the wing of Riverside Church along Claremont Avenue. It may have been, if memory serves, that the dinner guests were his seminar students and spouses or friends from the course on the Ecumenical Revolution. Many things for us were unsettled at the time, a time of existential fright and anxiety. The welcome, the warm welcome of that home, the dim awareness we had of who Brown was, who the Browns were, and their very humble circumstance, hospitality, and kindness to two and a half itinerant Methodists stands out after forty years. Robert McAfee Brown had a special reason for the dinner: He had invited a special guest, a colleague and friend whom he had met at Stanford but who was also now in New York, though he spent a part of each week in Boston. Our dinner guest had been invited to a professorship here at Boston University by then President John Silber, and, after some hesitation, as I understand it, he accepted. In a way, Brown's firm, lasting friendship with Wiesel, at least it seemed to me, reflected the friendship of the earlier generation between Reinhold Niebuhr and Abraham Heschel (who delivered Niebuhr's funeral eulogy in Stockbridge, Massachusetts, in 1971, just five years before we arrived at Union). So it was that we came to know Elie Wiesel.

Robert McAfee Brown's vision of the *oikoumene*[2] included Elie Wiesel, his celebrated dinner guest that snowy evening in 1979. By precept and example, then, Brown taught us to consider thinking and living in the same way. The later edition of *Night*[3] comes with a preface by Brown, after which Brown wrote his full book, *Elie Wiesel: Messenger to All Humanity*.[4] The book's dedication to Wiesel includes the following passage:

> I tried very hard, my friend, not to write this book. At every stage it seemed a tampering with things I had no right to touch. But because each exposure to your work moves me more deeply, I feel compelled to share a portion of what you have given me. To receive and not to share—that would be a denial of all that I have learned from you.
>
> You have said that to be a Jew means to testify; such must also be the obligation of a Christian. And you have taught us all—Jews, Christians, and all humanity—that before testifying ourselves, we must listen to the testimony of others. I have tried to listen to your testimony. And now I feel obligated . . . to testify.[5]

There is a *gracious* power in hospitality, like that which Professor Wiesel showed us in the Browns's residence, forty years ago. It lasts—the warmth and authenticity of it, they last. Said Unamuno: "Warmth, warmth, more warmth! for we die of cold, and not of darkness. It is not the night

---

2. From Greek: "the whole inhabited world"; the root of the English word "ecumenical."
3. Bantam, 1986.
4. University of Notre Dame Press, 1989.
5. Brown, *Elie Wiesel*, v. (Ellipsis in the original.)

that kills, but the frost."[6] Not the night of unknowing, but the frost of unloving—that is what kills.

Night

Speaking of night...

Through the eighties I pursued a PhD at McGill. As the dissertation was slowly writing itself—"We shall sell no wine before its time!"[7]—I began teaching in various schools. Montreal had an excellent film library, free and substantive, which I would raid on occasion for the course taught in community colleges along the border, up north. One perennial was a reel-to-reel film of Professor Wiesel.

Later still, the dissertation simmering nicely on the back burner for most of a decade—do not take my example—while teaching at Le Moyne College in Syracuse, we read *Night*, as so many have done over the years. The course prepared the way for it by use of another film—ancient technology—titled "On Ritual," whose lead figure was Jewish Theological Seminary Professor Neil Gillman (whose daughter Abigail is now our colleague here at BU). To paraphrase Gillman: *The central Jewish vision is the whole world made holy: all of life raised to its deepest and highest level.* The film follows the annual, weekly, and daily ritual life of a woman named Carol, one of the first women to enter the rabbinate in Conservative Judaism, and so teaches about Shabbat, and then about Rosh Hashanah, Yom Kippur, Booths, Hanukkah, Purim, and Passover. Ritual brings order to life.

Wiesel was the quintessential teacher. His books carried his voice out across the globe. Those who studied with him here regularly remember his remembrance of them. A Norwegian friend of mine vividly remembers Professor Wiesel getting him to gradually come out of his shell by telling funny stories. Our students at Le Moyne—a small Catholic school where most were the first in their families to attend college—connected with him from afar. In particular, the students always read and could always fully engage with Wiesel's book. I taught it by showing the points at which the Ten Commandments were engaged or broken (pages fifty, fifty-nine,

---

6. Unamuno, *Tragic Sense of Life*, 327.

7. This phrase is a slogan associated with Paul Masson California wines and made famous by a series of commercials featuring Orson Welles that aired from 1978 to 1981. The slogan implied that each wine was aged and refined to a certain point of quality before being released for sale.

seventy-one, seventy-three, ninety, and others). I never had a chance to ask him whether that was a fair way to teach the book, and whether he had the Decalogue in view for its structure. We learned from Wiesel and his book by raising questions. What is the central theme of the book? What is its weakest point? How do you describe the voice of the author? Which scene did you dislike most? What other writing does it recall? What would you ask the author if he were here today?

All of us—including and especially those who best remind us of our own best selves, like Professor Wiesel—are far more human than anything else. There is, I am sure, a full set of observations in loving critique that can and should be raised, and will be during the sessions offered in his honor this morning and afternoon. I wonder, for instance, just how inclusive his perspective was with regard to gay people. I wonder about his relationship with non-Orthodox Judaism. Like every sermon, every life has its points of challenge. But I, for one, have been deeply and lastingly influenced by the life and work of this one who lectured to us here thrice each autumn over forty years.

Franklin Littell, the first dean of Marsh Chapel, was not in the habit of mincing words. One ongoing application for those of us who have been seized by the confession of the church, who have been loved by the faithfulness of Christ, is to look again, to look long, to look hard at the Holocaust. We have yet to understand what happened *to Christianity* in the dark abyss, in the hellish, ghoulish fire of Auschwitz. Crucified, Judaism has risen from the dead. But what will become of Christianity? Will there arise a movement from religion to faith? Will there appear on the earth a religionless Christianity? Seventy years later, and the clock is ticking:

> Nazism was in no sense a revolt against "religion" and "spirituality." Neither was it "secularistic." Quite the contrary: in its central creed the party affirmed a devotion to *positives Christentum*. The *Führer* and other party orators made constant reference to "divine providence," "spiritual renewal," "moment of decision," "immortal destiny," "Christian front against materialism," and the like. Many of the party hymns were simply new words written to popular gospel songs, with the same brass bands marching and evoking from crowds the same emotional response. The key question, and here the issue of "heresy" arises, is why the millions of baptized and confirmed Christians had no sense that they were now responding to visions and programs antithetical to biblical faith.[8]

8. Littell, *Crucifixion of the Jews*, 69-70. (Italics in the original.)

Yet it was not, finally, the acute academic work of Littell and others that brought a fuller witness to and understanding of the Holocaust to the American conscience. That work was largely the influence of Wiesel. Just think back to the most horrific and jarring passage in *Night*:

> The SS seemed more preoccupied, more disturbed than usual. To hang a young boy in front of thousands of spectators was no light matter. The head of the camp read the verdict. All eyes were on the child. He was lividly pale, almost calm, biting his lips. The gallows threw its shadow over him.
>
> This time the [camp executioner] refused to act as executioner. Three SS replaced him.
>
> The three victims mounted together onto the chairs.
>
> The three necks were placed at the same moment within the nooses.
>
> "Long live liberty!" cried the two adults.
>
> But the child was silent.
>
> "Where is God? Where is He?" someone behind me asked.
>
> At a sign from the head of the camp, the three chairs tipped over.
>
> Total silence throughout the camp. On the horizon, the sun was setting.
>
> "Bare your heads!" yelled the head of the camp. His voice was raucous. We were weeping.
>
> "Cover your heads!"
>
> Then the march past began. The two adults were no longer alive. . . . But the third rope was still moving; being so light, the child was still alive . . .
>
> For more than half an hour he stayed there, struggling between life and death, dying in slow agony under our eyes. And we had to look him full in the face. He was still alive when I passed in front of him. . . .
>
> Behind me, I heard the same man asking:
>
> "Where is God now?"
>
> And I heard a voice within me answer him:
>
> "Where is He? Here He is—He is hanging here on this gallows. . . ."[9]

There is a *fierce* power in memory. Marcel Proust, with his madeleine moment, teaches us best: "A single minute released from the chronological order of time has re-created in us the human being similarly

---

9. Wiesel, *Night*, 70-71.

released . . . situated outside the scope of time, what could one fear from the future?"[10] These are "resurrections of the past."[11]

Vespers

From your own losses, your own experience of loss, you will perhaps know the power of kindness in the hour of grief. Our manner of grief, the way we grieve, is about the most personal thing about us—more individual than our eye color, height, skin pigmentation, gait, or fingerprint. Our friends and loved ones give us ourselves, and when we lose them we lose whole body parts, full and veritable pieces of our own most selves. For some, grief is light, for others, heavy; for some, tear filled, for others, "not something we cry about"; for some, long, and for others, short; for some, traumatic, for others, timely and then gone. At least we could be aware, for others, of other manners of grief, and respect what we can see and know and understand.

Our Gospel lesson today—neither taken from Saint Mark nor from "Q" but from the particular reservoir of Matthew's own sources (it is not found elsewhere)—stands out, up, and alone, and hardly needs interpretation. Is there not a poignancy in this pericope, in this recollection of a beloved teacher, not unlike that known in grief? The parable itself is as clear as a bell and as plain as the nose on your face (or, plainer still, as the nose on mine). *You have been loved, now love. Greatly have you been forgiven, so now greatly forgive.* "Man can have no more important privilege that to mediate to others the forgiveness which he himself experiences."[12]

In the weeks following my father's death seven years ago, there came many expressions of condolence, all of which were deeply appreciated, personally meaningful, and part of the healing, or the healing in grieving, or the health in grieving. It is a sacrament of sorts, grief is, as one friend said. At that time, June 2010, one of our leading choristers and dear friends worked here at the university. She was and is at the heart of Marsh Chapel to this date, even though she and her husband and children live in France. Her French is impeccable. Here, at the university, she worked as an assistant to Professor Elie Wiesel. At the time of my dad's death I received from her a note I cherish today, still:

---

10. Proust, *Remembrance of Things Past*, 2:996.
11. Proust, *Remembrance of Things Past*, 2:1111.
12. Buttrick, ed., *Interpreter's Bible*, 7:476.

Dean Hill—
Professor Wiesel asked me to send you the following message.
Ondine

Dear friend,
My deepest condolences. In our tradition we say: may you be spared further sorrow.
Elie Wiesel

There is a *poignant* power in kindness. Abraham Heschel: "Different are the languages of prayer, but the tears are all the same."[13]

Coda

Remember the words of Psalm 139.

> O Lord, you have searched me and known me.
> You know when I sit down and when I rise up;
>   you discern my thoughts from far away.
> You search out my path and my lying down
>   and are acquainted with all my ways.
> Even before a word is on my tongue,
>   O Lord, you know it completely.
> You hem me in, behind and before,
>   and lay your hand upon me.
> Such knowledge is too wonderful for me;
>   it is so high that I cannot attain it.
>
> Where can I go from your spirit?
>   Or where can I flee from your presence?
> If I ascend to heaven, you are there;
>   if I make my bed in Sheol, you are there.
> If I take the wings of the morning
>   and settle at the farthest limits of the sea,
> even there your hand shall lead me,
>   and your right hand shall hold me fast.
> If I say, "Surely the darkness shall cover me,
>   and night wraps itself around me,"
> even the darkness is not dark to you;
>   the night is as bright as the day,
>   for darkness is as light to you.

---

13. Heschel, *Insecurity of Freedom*, 180.

For it was you who formed my inward parts;
    you knit me together in my mother's womb.
I praise you, for I am fearfully and wonderfully made.
    Wonderful are your works;
that I know very well.
    My frame was not hidden from you,
when I was being made in secret,
    intricately woven in the depths of the earth.
Your eyes beheld my unformed substance.
In your book were written
    all the days that were formed for me,
    when none of them as yet existed.
How weighty to me are your thoughts, O God!
    How vast is the sum of them!
I try to count them—they are more than the sand;
    I come to the end—I am still with you.

O that you would kill the wicked, O God,
    and that the bloodthirsty would depart from me—
those who speak of you maliciously
    and lift themselves up against you for evil!
Do I not hate those who hate you, O Lord?
    And do I not loathe those who rise up against you?
I hate them with perfect hatred;
    I count them my enemies.
Search me, O God, and know my heart;
    test me and know my thoughts.
See if there is any wicked way in me,
    and lead me in the way everlasting.[14]

---

14. Ps 139:1-24, NRSVUE.

13

Hope That is Seen is Not Hope

Mark 8:27–34
Delivered at Boston University Marsh Chapel
September 16, 2018

Frontispiece

Hope that is seen is not hope. Who hopes for what he sees? We hope for what we do not see, and wait for it with patience.

Our denomination bade farewell to one of its great matriarchs this summer: Barbara Steen, who with her husband the Reverend Tom Steen mentored generations of clergy, especially regarding invitation in outreach and fellowship. Chuck Foster (*Educating Clergy*[1]) is an example. Their example teaches us about hope. In fact, Barb lived out the sense and substance of the Letter to the Romans, chapters 1, 3, 5, 8, 12, and 15.

What gracious good news to recall, in this era of racism, sexism, misogyny, xenophobia, irresponsibility, perversity, rapacity, and, especially, mendacity. Listen again to James, and to Mark.

---

1. Jossey-Bass, 2006.

The Tongue

If ever there were an age that could hear and appreciate the teaching of James about the tongue as a fire, it is our own. You know, the preacher here does not need to bring exegesis to bear, or give explanation for the wisdom proffered, or bring examples, many or few. We know from our evenings of listening to the cable news. We hear in our mornings of commuting with the radio on. We read and learn and inwardly digest what speech can do for ill. We are coming to a point where even James 3 is too tepid, too mild, to describe our national condition. At some point we will need to repair to Amos and drink the hard cold medicine of his teaching. When we without pause wreck the use of words, you do come to a time when words no longer work. You have stripped the gears. You have shredded the fabric. You have cut the muscle. And no one can speak the truth and no one can hear the truth any longer.

> The Lord was standing beside a wall built with a plumb line, with a plumb line in his hand. And the Lord said to me, "Amos, what do you see?" And I said, "A plumb line." Then the Lord said,
> "See, I am setting a plumb line
>   in the midst of my people Israel;
>   I will spare them no longer;
> the high places of Isaac shall be made desolate,
>   and the sanctuaries of Israel shall be laid waste,
> and I will rise against the house of Jeroboam with the sword."[2]
>
> The time is surely coming, says the Lord God,
> when I will send a famine on the land,
> not a famine of bread or a thirst for water,
> but of hearing the words of the Lord.
> They shall wander from sea to sea
> and from north to east;
> they shall run to and fro, seeking the word of the Lord,
> but they shall not find it.[3]

---

2. Amos 7:7-9, NRSVUE.

3. Amos 8:11-12, NRSVUE.

Mark 8:24–37

To renounce oneself, said John Chrysostom, is "to treat oneself as if one were another person."[4] Consider oneself as every day on the edge of death. Death makes us mortal. Facing death makes us human. We live at the intersection of present advent and future hope. What good is the greatest possession if there is no possessor to enjoy it? "Take up the cross" is a reference to the beginning of the journey, and the next part, "follow me," refers to the ongoing life of faith. Baptism first, you could say; Communion second, you could say.

We, like Peter, have aversion to suffering, as did Jesus in the garden of Gethsemane. Jesus is more than a prophet. But he is not less than a prophet.

Mark's harsh portrayal of Peter as "Satan"[5] is too much for Luke, who omits it later, and that reaction was probably not unique, for we can understand it too.

Hope that is seen is not hope. So your preachers this summer reminded you: Br. Whitney, Dr. Walton, Rev. Gaskell, Dr. Coleman, Rev. Donahue, and the dean, speaking about hope and righteousness, hope and freedom, hope and disappointment, hope and children, hope and lying, hope and listening, hope and the sweet aroma of the bread of life, hope and blending blue and red into purple (ok, maybe it was more like violet!), hope and faith.

Seek the Lost: Outreach

Barb and Tom Steen lived out of a desire to seek and to save the lost. That is old language, for sure. But it catches the fire and flavor of their—of her—faith. Many of us have had several helpings of faith, Sunday by Sunday. But for some, for some others, the first meal has yet to be served. That is where some of our youth work, some of our outreach and evangelism, some of our willingness to open the church to others who may at some point need community comes in. Asbury First United Methodist Church did this to national recognition in August this year.

Barb loved the camping programs at Watson Homestead and Casowasco. This summer, driving along Route 90, our granddaughter counted up the number of times she will be, and will have been, at Casowasco, this year and next. Many times. Barb would have smiled.

---

4. Marcus, *Mark*, 2:624.
5. Mark 8:33, NRSVUE.

We knew her many years ago, along the lakeshore of Owasco Lake, in the parlors of the building there aptly named "Galilee." We saw there the effect that can be had by loving community, caring presence, modulated teaching, all in a naturally beautiful setting.

One summer, toward the end of the season, we had as a camper a young man of about fifteen. He had never been to camp before. He was a rugged, stout fellow, who could and did pass the swim test, but barely. He was just full of life, and not overly attuned to boundaries. He had to sit out every now and then, but was quite affable about it, not minding the light discipline. He was such an exuberant fellow, it was hard not smile at his various antics. He was having a whale of time, all week long. I was working as the lifeguard, so I don't know how much Scripture he learned or how much praying he did, or how fully he could articulate his sense of faith. But he was every bit alive, all week long. And the meaning of life is in the living of life anyway, isn't it?

Come Friday, after lunch, our young friend disappeared. He did not show up for rest period, or the later class, or the swim at two o'clock. His counselors were rightly worried. We formed a search group, and trekked up to Mount Tabor, and hunted across the road in the Highlands, and looked through the gorge and the woods surrounding. No luck. By dinner we were plenty worried, even looking through the waterfront. Then, early that evening, I was walking up the railroad track to the south of the camp, still hunting. There he came, shuffling along. He told me why he ran away. He said that he did not want to go home. He said that the week had been the best one of his life, that he for once had friends, that he loved the hiking and meals and swimming, even the evening vespers. He just had never known anything like it. And he did not want to go home, to what he had to go home to. He told me about that, too.

That night, as he had some late supper, he came to something of realization. It wasn't so much that he could put everything into words. The gist of his thought was along the line of going home and making the best of it. But he would do it with memory of the week he had had, and that he would not forget, and he would not let the memory of the week fade. He would have to go home, but he could take something new home with him. Another way, another experience, another perspective, a little hope.

That is an example of what Barb and Tom aimed at, in that part of their ministry. A first helping of faith, shared genuinely, shared authentically, with those who had not yet had a chance to sit down at the table of fellowship and faith. It is what inspired her regular phone calls to our home in Rochester. Our growing-up children would hear, rattled out rapidly, "Hi, hon, Barb Steen here, how are you doing, how is school, is your mom there, thanks." She made her list of five or ten calls she would make every day, and she made them.

Welcome the Stranger: Fellowship

We left New York City suddenly, in 1979, to take a church in Ithaca, in the snows of February. Jan was ill, with child, and both the mother and the in utero baby had survived surgery for an ovarian cyst. The doctor at St. Elizabeth's in NYC had been unsure whether he could save either. Our conference and bishop had an open church in the neighborhood of Cornell University, and we had every need to be in place, be employed, be able to heal and prepare. Ordination—and with it, health insurance as a conference member—were months away, in mid-June, near the due date for the birth. As it happened, the child, our first, arrived two weeks late, a gift for some in the family, and a task for others.

We knew no one of our age, really, in the conference at that time. Those were hot, lonely months, with all the pure joy and utter confusion of parenthood's sudden arrival. The birth of our daughter, that day, July 5, 1979, was and remains the happiest day of my life. Whatever joy is, it is not something I can think about without the sight of that little beautiful baby, that beautiful young mother, and the delivery, which was deliverance, too. So we began to stumble around in ministry, writing sermons, making visits, trying to make sense of personal and church budgets, and a salary of eight thousand dollars a year, plus a house.

In early September, the phone rang in our little parsonage cottage in Ithaca, at the end of Forest Home Drive. "Hi, hon, Barb Steen here, how are you doing, how is the ministry, Ithaca has enough committees for everyone to be the chair of at least one, these people don't want faith they want a graduate course in religion—ugh!—is your wife there?" We knew Barb and Tom by reputation only, a part of which we were about to see in real time: their commitment to small groups, to welcome, to hospitality, to invitation. She called to invite us to a brunch two weeks hence in the Newfield parsonage, then occupied by Gary and Jeannie Judson. Later in ministry, our Syracuse predecessor Rev. Wayne Archer (his wife a Fenton, of Fenton glass), reminded us that the Newfield church burned down during his ministry there. Oddly, the district superintendent had said, "Archer, light a fire under that church." Well, Wayne also had served a church in Pennsylvania that hard burned, hence his nickname, "the arson parson." But Newfield UMC was rebuilt, and its parsonage, as the older ones do, had a big parlor.

Barb had gathered a dozen twenty-something couples, including the Judsons and the Hills, who didn't know each other from Adam's house cat, for a meal. Half or more had little babies in tow. We sang and prayed a little, ate a little more, and laughed a whole lot more about the oddities of life, young adult life, parenthood, ministry, and the loneliness lurking behind and above and underneath them all. She gave us ourselves by giving us to each other. *She gave us ourselves, by giving us to each other.* We came alive. The next week, the phone rang. "Hi, hon, Barb Steen here, how is the ministry, how is life, how is that beautiful little "Emly," how are your folks Marcia and Irv, wasn't that a great brunch at the Judson's, is Jan there?"

From that one gathering friendships formed. One minister then took me to lunch. Another suggested a round of golf. A third saw my car and told to me to come over so that he could teach me how to change the brake pads: "You don't want to spend money on that. You can't afford it on eight thousand dollars a year. I'll help you." A fourth came and preached on Christmas Eve, making reference, in earshot of Rudolph, to the blessed taste of venison. Thanks to Bob, to Duane, to Gary, and to Dale. Tom Steen himself got me into a clergy study of the Psalms that lasted two years, until we moved north.

The habits of visitation, the habits of welcome, the habits of outreach, the habits of hospitality, the habits of Christian charity and love, all so dearly central to any genuine form of ministry, are not necessarily permanent gifts. They have to be remembered. To be remembered, they have to be modeled. To be modeled, they have to be practiced. I give you: Barb Steen.

Peter Berger (*A Rumor of Angels*[6]) reminded us that the very sense we have of lasting, earthly injustice, of wrongs not and never made right, a real and palpable sentiment, is itself a rumor of something more. Which we cannot see, of course, and of which we do not know, of course. But maybe a heavenly breakfast will again be served, at which the table will seat the resurrection of the just. We hope for what we do not see.

---

6. Doubleday, 1969.

14

Hope is the Negation of Negation

Lectionary Texts: Nehemiah, Psalm, 1 Corinthians, Luke
Delivered at Boston University Marsh Chapel
January 24, 2019

We are living through a negative time.

Before dawn, aroused by a dream, you awake, it may be. In the mind clutter of the dream you stand in community, listening for a holy word, it may be. Or you walk, mesmerized by the beauty of a beach or a mountain vista, it may be. Or you otherwise sense the tug of a common good, a common desire, it may be. In the mind clutter of the dream, too, you may wait to hear something, it may be. Before dawn, in the moonlight. Drowsiness returns, and you return to the arms of Morpheus, god of sleep. But the time to rise comes along soon enough, and you take stock again, and you realize again what time it is.

We are living through a negative time.

For some, the negation is a chosen, intentional negation of inherited forms of public speech, of national discourse, of governmental responsibility, of encroaching and overweening statism, of political correctness, of international order and regular borders—a time to pluck up, a time to pluck up what is planted. Or so one supposes.

HOPE IS THE NEGATION OF NEGATION

For others, many others, the negation is a consequence of all this and more, and amounts to a frightening, even terrifying daily rending of the garment of national life, the rending of the garment of civil society, the rending of the garment of compassionate care for the young, the poor, the sick, and the old; the steady destruction of treaties, alliances, and agreements, welling up from a steady disdain for treaties, alliances, and agreements; a rending of the garments of courtesies developed over a long time to shelter ourselves from our worst selves; the standard (if sometimes honored in the breach) shared, common rejection of misogyny, racism, sexism, xenophobia, greed, pride, sloth, and falsehood. And, in their place, another kind of clothing: a laughing joy in slaughtering the truth, and a willingness to do so by fulsome mendacity in the small and in the large.

Whether you, with some, celebrate such, or whether you, with many, abhor it, now over the last few years it has become clear: we are living through a time of negation.

You arise in the morning, in a wonderment, a dark wonder. Will someone be given the nuclear car keys, with which to incinerate another land? Will the government return again to potential "fire and fury"[1] against a foreign people? Will the lax tax on the rich bankrupt government protections of the poor? Will the clearly emerging authoritarianism become patent and fulsome on the strength of a manufactured crisis at a border, or far away, or, most possibly, in cyberspace?

You brush your teeth, pour your coffee, turn on the news, and, amid a wonderment, a dark wonder, you do wonder: Did I ever think I would live to see the day that my beloved country—to which I have pledged allegiance since kindergarten, for which I acquired a Selective Service card, to which I have paid taxes (now grudgingly, now willingly) over many decades, on whose account I have voted every year since the years of the silent majority and that Methodist minister's son from North Dakota, land where my father has died, land of the pilgrim's pride—be held hostage like Jayme Closs,[2] a thirteen-year-old girl in Wisconsin, like her the whole country bound, gagged, hidden under the single bed and held hostage to the megalomania of an imperial, increasingly authoritarian government; to a complicit citizenry that cannot yet fully reckon, neither to reject nor

---

1. A reference to a statement made about North Korea in 2017 by then President Trump.

2. Jayme Closs, missing since her parents were found fatally shot on October 15, 2018, was found alive on January 10, 2019. According to reports, her captor at times kept her confined under a bed.

recant the 2016 tragedy;[3] to a Senate whose every murmur now carries the middle name Faust for its deal with the devil in aid of paternalistic judges and capitalism gone wild and a willful blindness to the roaring, rising tide of exclusion, falsehood, selfishness, incivility, unkindness, and greed?

Each morning brings a darker wonder, and you wonder how this can ever have anything other than the bleakest outcome. We are living through a negative time. In our time, we are hostages to negativity, living through a most perilously negative time, with no exit readily or easily in sight. Some of us may realize that we will be dead, even long dead, before the blood is fully spilled and washed, before the dawn comes, before a return to the country's rightful mind. We are living through a time of negation.

For a post-Christian culture and society, the next question, then, is not what it is right now and right here in Christian worship—the question of the possibility of preaching—not what it is right now and right here in the spirit of Christian community, not what it is in this venerable pulpit and other siblings to it across the land. As a whole, as a culture, we are no longer—if we ever fully were—rooted in or grounded by hope, no longer grounded by the promise of the Gospel, if we ever were so. For society as a whole, the basic question of this moment—the preaching moment—is not, for the culture, a big or even serious question at all. The symbols of faith have grown cold in a culture, in a land that is Godforsaken, or, better put, simply forsaken. So, our problem (or mine, in this moment)—the prospect of preaching, the problem of the possibility of preaching, the problem of how to sing the Lord's song in a foreign land, the problem of how to preach a word of faith in a pastoral voice toward a common hope, the problem of hope itself, in its realest, truest form, faith working through love—is not that of our culture. The radio program "Wait Wait. . . Don't Tell Me!" is not waiting for the telling of a true hope. It is not perseverating about whether there can be, or will be, in our time, any preaching worthy of the name, let alone who on earth will deign to try to do it, Sunday by Sunday. No, only the bitter biblical herb of "hope deferred [that] maketh the heart sick"[4] has any natural or easy purchase in our nonreligious age. Yes, we are living through a negative time.

In our time, hope—if it has any hope in it—is itself negation. A cheery, light, pseudo inner life, a false gaiety, a *que será, será* is not hope. It is false hope. Some listening today will find the depiction of negation offered this

---

3. A reference to the outcome of the 2016 US presidential election.
4. Prov 13:12, KJV.

morning to be too negative. You may be people my age and older. Some listening today, though, will find the depiction of negation to be not negative enough. You may be people my children's age, some 35 percent of whom now identify, or non-identify, as "nones": those of no religion at all, but who will have to clean up much of the mess of these years. No. "Hope that is seen is not hope."[5] That is in the Bible. "Who hopes for what one already sees?"[6] That, too, is in the Bible. "We hope for what we do not see"[7] (the key, for once, is in the adverb: "not"). That is in the Bible, too. In our time, hope—if it has any hope in it—is itself pure negation.

[Pause.]

And in that negation, it may be, is the lone location, just now, for preaching. Hope is the negation—of negation. *Hope is the negation—of negation.*

Hope is the negation of prideful overconfidence in our national or personal histories. One lasting good in a negative time is that it leaves little space for high horses ridden and deadly assumptions hugged. Authoritarianism can evolve, right here, just now, all the glories of the Freedom Trail notwithstanding. *Authoritarianism can evolve, right here, just now, all the glories of the Freedom Trail notwithstanding.*

So, Dietrich Bonhoeffer: "God would have us know that we must live as men [and women] who manage our lives without him. The God who is with us is the God who forsakes us . . . Before God and with God we live without God."[8]

Hope is the negation of our lazy, slothful spirituality—what a strange, odd, unbiblical word. Hope is the negation of our lazy, slothful unwillingness, on the left, to be politically involved (to go to meetings, to go to meetings, to go to meetings), and, on the right, our refusal—now that the evidence is in—to recant what we chose, for whatever reason, to do three years ago. That negation comes to gruesome light, even in a twilight hope.

Hope is the negation of our falsehood, our capacity to somehow look past or forgive or minimize the lying, the mendacity, the screaming falsehood of our naively authoritarian leadership. Hope is the negation of the

---

5. "For in hope we were saved. Now hope that is seen is not hope, for who hopes for what one already sees?" Rom 8:24, NRSVUE.

6. Rom 8:24, NRSVUE.

7. Rom 8:25, NRSVUE.

8. Bonhoeffer, *Letters and Papers from Prison*, 360. (Bracketed words reflect an addition to the gender-specific language found in the original.)

dark wonder. It is that which makes things clear, or clearer, at dawn. In the light of hope.

Let us boil this down to daily life, if we may. It is almost inevitable, you human being you, that in the age of negativity, in the maelstrom of unlimited negative informational bombardment, of windswept rain soaking every daily pore—it is inevitable that you will now and then be depressed. You will be. That you will now and then be worried. You will be. That you will now and then be haunted by bad memories and dark dreams. You will be. You cannot avoid it. Forgive yourself. Forgive yourself. Forgive yourself. There. That feels good, or at least better. *Hope walks by faith, not by sight.*[9] Faith is a walk in the dark. Faith is the power to withstand what we cannot understand, to embrace hope that negates what it cannot eliminate. What you can do is this: listen to the gospel, which is the negation of negation by hope, the negation of acedia by hope, the negation of depression and worry and anxiety by hope. Not the elimination, no—the negation. Hope will give you a breakfast ounce of courage. Hope will give you a noonday morsel of anger. Hope will give you a twilight flicker of faith. Because hope stands as the very negation of negation. It is not something, hope, that you or I can concoct or control or conjure. Hope stands in the pulpit, say, and speaks to us, say, and does so without fear or favor, without quiver or conceit, say, and utters a word of faith (take heart) in a pastoral voice (I am with you) toward a common hope (you are a child of God).

Hope—a sense that things are wrong and can be right-wised—is what gives us the angry courage, the courageous anger, to rise up, to resist out of a tradition of principled resistance dating back to Amos of Tekoa in the eighth century BCE, to struggle, to lose, to be defeated, and to get up again. Hope is the raising of the dead.

Jürgen Moltmann:

> To recognize the event of the resurrection of Christ is therefore to have a hopeful and expectant knowledge of this event. It means recognizing in this event the latency of that eternal life which in the praise of God arises from the negation of the negative, from the raising of the one who was crucified and the exaltation of the one who was forsaken. It means assenting to the tendency towards resurrection of the dead in this event of the raising of the one. It means following the intention of God by entering into the dialectic of suffering and dying in expectation of eternal life and of resurrection.

9. A reference to 2 Cor 5:7, NRSVUE.

> ... Thus the Spirit is the power to suffer in participation in the mission and the love of Jesus Christ, and is in this suffering the passion for what is possible, for what is coming and promised in the future of life, of freedom and of resurrection. ... In all our acts we are sowing in hope.[10]

Before dawn, aroused by a dream, you awake, it may be. In the mind clutter of the dream you stand in community listening for a holy word, it may be. This is the gospel of Nehemiah, that there is a Holy Scripture, strange yet audible. Or you walk, mesmerized by the beauty of a beach or a mountain vista, it may be. This is the gospel of the psalmist, in the most beautiful of all one hundred and fifty psalms—"all nature sings, and round me rings the music of the spheres."[11] Or you otherwise sense the tug of a common good, a common desire, it may be. This is the gospel of the Epistle, Spirit known for what it does for the common good. In the mind clutter of the dream, too, you may wait to hear something, it may be. This is, here in Luke, Jesus preaching at home but not welcomed, preaching the divine favor for the poor, not just the poor in spirit; for the oppressed, not just the figuratively oppressed; for the captive, not just the philosophically captive. Before dawn, in the moonlight.

Hope negates what it cannot eliminate. Hope is the negation of negation. Said Paul, "Look, I will tell you a mystery!"[12] Said John, "Where I am, there you may be also."[13] Said Paul, "The trumpet will sound."[14] Said John, "You know the way . . . where I am going."[15] Said Paul, "The dead will be raised."[16] Said John, "I am the way and the truth and the life."[17] Said Paul, "In a moment, in the twinkling of an eye."[18]

> He unrolled the scroll and found the place where it was written:
> "The Spirit of the Lord is upon me,
>   because he has anointed me
>   to bring good news to the poor.

---

10. Moltmann, *Theology of Hope*, 211, 212-13.
11. Babcock, "God," no. 72, st. 1.
12. 1 Cor 15:51, NRSVUE.
13. John 14:3, NRSVUE.
14. 1 Cor 15:52, NRSVUE.
15. John 14:4, NRSVUE.
16. 1 Cor 15:52, NRSVUE.
17. John 14:6, NRSVUE.
18. 1 Cor 15:52, NRSVUE.

> He has sent me to proclaim release to the captives
> and recovery of sight to the blind,
> to set free those who are oppressed,
> to proclaim the year of the Lord's favor."

And he rolled up the scroll . . . and began to say to them, "Today this scripture has been fulfilled in your hearing."[19]

---

19. Luke 4:17-21, NRSVUE.

15

Liberal Hope

Matthew 23:1–12
Delivered at Boston University Marsh Chapel
November 1, 2020: All Saints' Day

WE ARE TAUGHT, IN today's gospel, to practice what we preach.

Geese return to their nesting place, that place chosen for laying eggs and sheltering the young. Every year, geese come home to their birth place, as my lake friend tells me. They are loud this year, louder than one remembers, calling, *glampa, glampa, glampa*. The dark skies and then the lake fill with them as they find their place of nesting and some fish for lunch or dinner.

They may have come from the northwest, perhaps an hour or three earlier swinging past the burial plot of Harriet Tubman in Auburn, New York. She, with her faith and pistol, brought liberal hope to hearts of enslaved people, hiking along the dark riverbed of the Susquehanna, and, for many, on to that lasting neighborly land of hope just across the Saint Lawrence. She is interred near Lincoln's opponent become ally, William Seward, who bought us Alaska. Along fly the geese, in their autumn season of travel. We too are itinerants, you and I, unfeathered but on the move, moving into a new chapter this coming week.

The geese, spread out in V formations, may then cross by the edge of Cooperstown, resting on the head of Abner Doubleday's handsome statue, an hour or so north of Pennsylvania, that hotly contested region of Quakers and farmers, not far from Philadelphia where Benjamin Franklin gave us the post office. Remember Franklin's warning: you have "a republic, if you can keep it."[1] Or, in addition, he might have said, *You have a post office, if you can keep it.*

Ah, the geese, reminding us of the season, the time. Others of their feather will fly along the Hudson River, too, perhaps near Tivoli, on that river's bank, where my grandfather is buried. He left me a gold pocket watch, which one day I will give to my grandson, Charles Robert. An hour of extra sleep on All Saints' Sunday may allow us a reach of memory toward those no longer among the church militant, but now among the church triumphant. That riverbank cemetery also holds our great uncle Myron, of murky but mythic family memory, who fought in the war to end all wars, then came home through Boston in 1918 and contracted influenza during the epidemic, as we were regularly told growing up, and died in the second wave, March 1919. Probably there were some back then who said of that plague: *it will all just go away, like magic.* Except it didn't. And, it won't. He left a canteen, without a jacket, dented and silver colored, which came my way for camping trips and was lost, left somewhere up Mount Marcy in the Adirondacks one autumn. His grave is a hundred miles from our dear lady whose liberal hope, tattered but alive, still rings out in the harbor: "Give me your tired, your poor, your huddled masses yearning to breathe free, the wretched refuse of your teeming shore. Send these, the homeless, the tempest-tost to me, I lift my lamp beside the golden door!"[2]

Coming due east along Route 90, you nearly drove past New Lebanon without stopping, so eager were you to get back into the Commonwealth of Massachusetts, and mesmerized by the geese overhead. Here is the ghost, the shade, the specter of Mother Ann Lee and the Shaking Quakers, eschewing body for the sake of spirit, at the edge of the mountains, such communal liberal hope they had, a greathearted willingness to practice what they preached. They remembered the height of Jesus's hope. Do we?

1. Franklin's quote was directed to Elizabeth Willing Powel, who on the final day of the 1787 Constitutional Convention approached Franklin to ask: "Well, Doctor, what have we got, a republic or a monarchy?" The exchange was recorded by James McHenry, Maryland delegate to the Convention. See: Miller, *Unfolding History* (blog), Library of Congress.

2. Lazarus, "New Colossus," lines 10-14.

> But I say to you who are listening: Love your enemies; do good to those who hate you; bless those who curse you; pray for those who mistreat you. If anyone strikes you on the cheek, offer the other also, and from anyone who takes away your coat do not withhold even your shirt. Give to everyone who asks of you, and if anyone takes away what is yours, do not ask for it back again. Do to others as you would have them do to you.
>
> If you love those who love you, what credit is that to you? For even sinners love those who love them. If you do good to those who do good to you, what credit is that to you? For even sinners do the same. If you lend to those from whom you expect to receive payment, what credit is that to you? Even sinners lend to sinners, to receive as much again. Instead, love your enemies, do good, and lend, expecting nothing in return. Your reward will be great, and you will be children of the Most High, for he himself is kind to the ungrateful and the wicked. Be merciful, just as your Father is merciful.[3]

All these nesting places of hope, places of recollection of our own best selves. Who do you mean to be, at your most hopeful? Are we lovers anymore? Who do you mean to be, as your own most self? It is a riveting question, is it not, this very week.

You could come further east, along Route 90 or even Route 20 or even bluer highways, winding into the Berkshires, which always seem dreamlike with or without the white snow frosting. Fewer geese, but some still, wending their way, flying on, calling out, *glampa, glampa, glampa.*

Here is Stockbridge, Massachusetts, home to Jonathan Edwards, on whose life and work we preached here at Marsh Chapel a few winters ago. He who is too much remembered for sinners in the hands of an angry God and too little recalled for his sense of the holy, his love of nature, and his rendering of Scripture. Here is the Stockbridge church, geese on the lawn, where in 1971 Abraham Heschel gave the eulogy for Reinhold Niebuhr. Think of that ecumenical, interreligious, capacious hope, a liberal hope, a hope in what we have in common. Niebuhr asked Heschel to preach at his funeral. Stockbridge is a town like those back a bit west along the Mohawk, in which we were raised. Raised by a community. Look back at the people: an insurance man, a Latin teacher, a Scout executive, a musician, the owner of a heater company, a minister, several farmers. All of the same Grand Old Party, by the way. They taught honesty. They practiced civility. They formed a creed around courtesy. They made space for charity. They prized example.

---

3. Luke 6:27-36, NRSVUE.

They had no truck with, or patience for, mendacity or perversity or self-aggrandizement. They listened to what people said, but they watched what people did. Particularly leaders. Like it says in the Bible today, practice what you preach.[4] Boy, that was a long time ago, wasn't it? Not just in years, but in habits of the heart.

We need, again, their balance, honesty, and hope. We need to recover their magnanimity. We need the blue sky of aspiration that they saw. For such a thick cloud comes from a theological weather system in which the cold front of wrong has chased out the warm front of right; in which the low pressure of the fall has displaced the high pressure of creation; in which the radical postmodern apotheosis of difference has silenced the liberal, late modern openness to shared experience, to promise and future, to common faith, common ground, common hope, liberal hope; in which the creation is seen from the cavern of the fall, not the fall from the prairie of creation; in which we have forgotten what the geese remember. Their nesting place, their birthright, their place and spirit of origin.

This is a pastoral problem. It is not just, or mainly, a political conflict. It is a theological contrast. It is not a matter of church coloration or religious style, it is a matter of creation, of God's creation and the truth about creative goodness. Just how balanced is our balance between creation and fall? And God saw all that God made, and it was good. Not perfect, but good. There are a lot of things wrong. But. There are a lot of things right, too. How do we find that balance?

We locate that balance in a magnanimous hope. As the theologian said, "Thus the Spirit is the power to suffer in participation in the mission and the love of Jesus Christ, and is in this suffering the passion for what is possible, for what is coming and promised in the future of life, of freedom and of resurrection. . . . In all our acts we are sowing in hope."[5]

It is two hours from the river to the ocean, from the Hudson to the Atlantic. In and across those two hours, say, as the crow or even as the goose flies, there lies a great deal of our shared history. If you get to Boston, come by Marsh Chapel, where there is a monument to Martin Luther King Jr. I walked past it again this morning. It is mute, silent, and yet its very stone cries out, its marble makes music and sings, for those with ears to hear. It is a statue that points to a liberal hope, and so points away from much

---

4. "Do whatever they teach you and follow it, but do not do as they do, for they do not practice what they teach." Matt 23:3, NRSVUE.

5. Moltmann, *Theology of Hope*, 212-13.

of our experience in the last four years. Yes, it points to justice—though justice is not the deepest heart of the gospel, of faith, of religion, or of that monument. It is a part, but not the heart. The heart belongs to . . . *another word, another gospel word.* Not one in opposition to the first, but one in tension and tandem with the first, and one outpacing the first. The heart of the gospel is love, and love is the marrow of the liberal hope, one true hope worthy of the name. King can teach us still: There is a liberal hope in the sometime radical practice of loving-kindness.

Last summer, I was asked to offer a thought about love and transformation for the final portion of our summer devotions. My friend from Yale, Gene Outka, once helped me think about this. He reminded us that Martin Luther King Jr. advanced a compelling version of love, including love of enemies. In this affirmation, King distinguished agape from eros, or romantic love, and from philia, or friendship, as follows:

> *Agape* is more than romantic love, *agape* is more than friendship. Agape is understanding, creative, redemptive good will to all [people]. It is an overflowing love which seeks nothing in return . . . So that when one rises to love on this level, he loves [others] not because he likes them, not because their ways appeal to him, but he loves every [one] because God loves him. And he rises to the point of loving the person who does an evil deed while hating the deed that the person does. I think this is what Jesus meant when he said "love your enemies." I'm very happy that he didn't say like your enemies, because it is pretty difficult to like some people. Like is sentimental, and it is pretty difficult to like someone bombing your home; it is pretty difficult to like somebody threatening your children; it is difficult to like congressmen who spend all of their time trying to defeat civil rights. But Jesus says love them, and love is greater than like.[6]

Hear good news: In Jesus "there is a new creation, a new man [and woman], a new life, a new age, a new covenant."[7] In Jesus there is a hopeful creation, a hopeful man and woman, a hopeful life, a hopeful age, a hopeful covenant.

In a moment we will hear again the ancient liturgy for Eucharist. We are not together to receive, together, the bread and cup. But we are together in relationship, by memory, in hope, through prayer. And with a little

---

6. King Jr., *Testament of Hope*, 46-47. (Bracketed words reflect changes from gender-specific language found in the original.)

7. Albright and Mann, trans., *Matthew*, xxviii.

imagination, with eyes closed and hearts open, we might allow the familiar, ancient prayers of communion to bring us into communion.

So, travel with a little imagination. Imagine Eucharist at Marsh Chapel. Stand to sing . . . Pause to reflect . . . Step out into the aisle . . . Look at and look past Abraham Lincoln and Francis Willard . . . Receive cup and bread, bread and cup . . . Kneel at the altar to pray . . . Stand in communion with the communion of saints on this All Saints' Day . . . Here is the bread and cup of friendship . . .

Imagine, if you are willing, your own funeral, say, right here, and a congregation reciting together a creed, a psalm, a hymn, a poem. Imagine, if you are willing, a congregation currently in diaspora, but just now, by the word spoken, a gathered and thus addressable community—you and I and all, together.

And let us practice what we preach. Come home, this All Saints' Day. Come home to the place of your nesting, the place of your birth, the place of your baptism, the place of your taking wing, taking flight—your nesting place. It is a fine place to visit, as the winter comes on and you look for warmth, for health, for nourishment, for salvation. It is a little lake named love, a nesting place for the liberal hope.

We await a liberal hope—a hope:

That our warming globe, caught in climate change, will be cooled by cooler heads and calmer hearts and careful minds.

That our dangerous world, armed to the teeth with nuclear proliferation, will find, through deft leadership, peace toward nuclear détente.

That our culture, in part awash in hooliganism, will find again the language and the song and the spirit of the better angels of our nature.

That our country, fractured by massive inequality between rich children and poor children, will rise up and make education, free education, available to all children, poor and rich.

That our nation, fractured by flagrant unjust inequality between rich and poor children, will stand up and make health care, free health care, available to all children, poor and rich.

That our schools, colleges, and universities will balance a love of learning with a sense of meaning, a pride in knowledge with a respect for goodness, a drive for discovery with a regard for recovery.

That our families, torn apart by abuse and distrust and anger and jealousy and unkindness, will social distance this Thanksgiving and, with or without a common meal, will show kindness and pity to one another.

That our decisions in life about our callings, how we are to use our time and spend our money—how we make a life, not just a living—will be illumined by grace and generosity.

That our grandfathers and mothers, in their age and infirmity, will receive care and kindness that accords with the warning to honor father and mother that your own days be long upon the earth.[8]

We await a liberal hope, finally—a hope not of this world, but of this world as a field of formation for another; not just creation but new creation; not just life but eternal life; not just health but salvation; not just heart but soul; not just earth, but heaven.

Now—from Auburn to Cooperstown to Albany to Stockbridge to Boston—like geese in flight, we have come. They call to us: *glampa, glampa, glampa*. Maybe we want to pray. What shall we pray? Shall we pray in words Martin Luther King used in August of 1963? Shall we pray in words with music that Aretha Franklin sang in January of 2009? Shall we pray time-honored words written just down the street in Boston, the nesting place of America, the place of birth for both goose and gander, your words—from 1831 and a children's concert at Park Street Church and the pen of an Andover Newton Seminary graduate, Samuel Francis Smith—your words, Boston, your hymn, Boston, your psalm of liberal hope?

> My country, 'tis of thee,
> sweet land of liberty,
> of thee I sing:
> land where my fathers died,
> land of the pilgrims' pride,
> from every mountainside
> let freedom ring.
>
> . . .
>
> Let music swell the breeze,
> and ring from all the trees
> sweet freedom's song:
> let mortal tongues awake,
> let all that breathe partake,
> let rocks their silence break,
> the sound prolong.[9]

---

8. A reference to Exod 20:12, NRSVUE.

9. Smith, "My Country, 'Tis of Thee," st. 1 and 4. The song was first performed in public on July 4, 1831, at a children's Independence Day celebration at Boston's Park Street Church.

16

A Sermon on the Mound

Mark 6:1–13
Delivered at Boston University Marsh Chapel
July 4, 2021

"So they went out and proclaimed that all should repent."[1]

Winthrop

OUT ON THE MASSACHUSETTS Bay, in the autumn of 1630, Governor Jonathan Winthrop spoke to frightened pilgrims, half of whom would be dead and gone before spring. One can try to imagine the rolling of the frigate in the surf out on the Atlantic. One can feel the salt breeze, the water wind of the sea—not too very far from the nave of Marsh Chapel. The governor, in his sermon for the day, is brief: "We must consider that we shall be a city upon a hill. The eyes of all people are upon us, so that if we shall deal falsely with our God in this work we have undertaken, and so cause Him to withdraw His present help from us, we shall be made a story and a byword

---

1. Mark 6:12, NRSVUE.

through the world."[2] A remarkable, truly remarkable warning, to our country at the moment of its inception.

Lincoln

It is a cold day in early March 1865. Fourscore and eight years after Independence, the nation has indeed become, as Winthrop prophesied in his Boston sermon, "a story and byword through the world." Six hundred thousand men will have died by the time Lee and Grant meet at Appomattox—approximately one death for every ten slaves forcibly brought to the New World. This day in March, Mr. Lincoln delivers his own sermon to the gathered congress—a congress that is for once, we may assume, chastened. It is Lincoln's "Second Inaugural":

> The Almighty has His own purposes . . . Fondly do we hope—fervently do we pray—that this mighty scourge of war may speedily pass away. Yet, if God wills that it continue until all the wealth piled by the bondsman's two hundred and fifty years of unrequited toil shall be sunk, and until every drop of blood drawn by the lash shall be paid by another drawn with the sword, as was said three thousand years ago, so still it must be said, "The judgments of the Lord are true and righteous altogether."
>
> With malice toward none; with charity for all; with firmness in the right, as God gives us to see the right—let us strive on to finish the work we are in: to bind up the nation's wounds; to care for him who shall have borne the battle, and for his widow and his orphan; to do all which may achieve and cherish a just and lasting peace among ourselves, and with all nations.[3]

Into the next decade the state of Mississippi will spend 20 percent of its annual budget, each year, for artificial limbs. Lincoln himself will die within weeks of the inaugural address.

A remarkable warning, a presidential warning, a sermonic warning.

King

Now we witness another gathering, and we hear another sermon. A hundred more years have passed. It is August 28, 1963, a sweltering day in the

2. Winthrop, "Model of Christian Charity," 246.
3. Lincoln, *Speeches*, 360-61.

nation's capital. Thousands of women and men have gathered within earshot of Lincoln's memorial, within earshot of his "Second Inaugural." By some measure, too, they have gathered within the reverberated cautions given by Winthrop out in our Boston Bay. They have come—maybe some of you were there—"with firmness in the right, as God gives to see the right," to strive to finish the work. A Baptist preacher captures the moment in ringing oratory: "I have a dream that one day on the red hills of Georgia, sons of former slaves and sons of former slave-owners will be able to sit down together at the table of brotherhood."[4]

Remarkable, truly remarkable words.

Winthrop. Lincoln. King. 1630. 1865. 1963. These are three of the greatest sermons ever preached in our country's history. *Do we notice that not one of them was delivered in a church?* Yet they all interpret the church's gospel. They all apply the gospel of Christ, and its ringing command in Mark 6, to the land of the free and the home of the brave.

Winthrop. Lincoln. King. They believed in God's presence. They trusted—through times of what can only be called terror—in God's favor. And mostly, they thought and felt and *thoughtfelt* and *feltthought* that persons, even they themselves, had roles to play in the divine human drama. They spoke in harmony with Jesus's challenge: "So they went out and proclaimed that all should repent."[5] They spoke in a way that awakened the hearer.

All three knew tragedy, as we have again this year, with six hundred thousand souls gone to glory; as we have again this winter, with mendacity and violence used to usurp electoral outcomes; as we have again this week, with another tower—like that of the biblical Siloam—coming down in Miami Beach, for whose victims and families we truly do grieve. They warned of tragedy, they endured tragedy, they honestly acknowledged tragedy. What Winthrop prophesied, and what Lincoln witnessed, and what King addressed is, to some degree, our national tragedy still. Though there has been progress, we still judge far too much by the color of skin and not by the content of character. As my predecessor Dr. Robert Cummings Neville well said, from this pulpit one Sunday years ago: "Probably the deepest issue in our society is racism, a poisonous stain that mixes evil into the very best of our inventive history of democracy and our love of freedom."[6]

---

4. King Jr., *I Have a Dream*, 104.

5. Mark 6:12, NRSVUE.

6. From the author's memory. Dr. Neville was dean of Marsh Chapel from 2003 to 2006, and frequently preached from its pulpit.

A Sermon on the Mound

But God has not left us, nor does God abandon God's children. God works through human hearts to bind up the nation's wounds. It is the preaching of the gospel of Jesus Christ that can bring peace. The church has nothing better to do, nothing other to do, nothing more important to do, nothing else to do than to preach. "So they went out and proclaimed that all should repent."[7]

And some of the best preaching happens beyond church. Some is spoken, and some is lived. Said Benjamin Franklin, teaching the two values he thought important—industry and frugality: "None preaches better than the ant, and he says nothing."[8]

Here is one saving story from which, over time, we may gain strength and insight for our common story, poetry, and preaching. For what Walt Whitman said about poetry is doubly true for the gospel itself: "The United States themselves are essentially the greatest poem. . . . Here at last is something in the doings of man that corresponds with the broadcast doings of the day and night."[9] And: "Really great poetry is always . . . the result of a national spirit, and not the privilege of a polish'd and select few . . . the strongest and sweetest songs yet remain to be sung."[10] *The strongest and sweetest songs yet remain to be sung.*

Looking back forty years to Jesus's ministry, our Gospel writer has recalled in stylized memory a powerful teaching moment. All the Gospels, including our text, were formed—*formed*—in the white heat of early church life, when the hand of death threatened a frightened church, perhaps in Rome, perhaps in the year 70 BCE.

This is the meaning of a sermon: to wake us up from a deathlike sleep, to take us out of the arms of Morpheus, god of sleep. With Mark's frightened early church, we may again hear good news. Sometimes what seems like death—think of the Gospel last Sunday—is merely napping. For example, this holiday weekend, we may want to remember . . .

---

7. Mark 6:12, NRSVUE.
8. Franklin, "Poor Richard's Almanac, 1735," 319.
9. Whitman, *Leaves of Grass*, 488.
10. Whitman, *Leaves of Grass*, 536.

Branch Rickey

Next year we shall pass the seventy-fifth anniversary of Jackie Robinson's entrance into major league baseball. Decades ago, the armed forces were still legally segregated. So were public schools. So was America in 1947, when a teetotal, Bible-quoting, Republican, Methodist layman from Ohio—Mr. Branch Rickey—brought racial integration to major league baseball. Who remembers, today, this lone ranger type who spent much of a lifetime working for one transformation? Rickey was taught the gospel in a church where there was to be no separation between a deep personal faith and an active social involvement. He was formed at a small Methodist school, Ohio Wesleyan, one of whose presidents, Bishop James Bashford, peers down on us today from the beautiful stained glass of Marsh Chapel. Rickey was one of those people who just never heard that "it can't be done." For thirty years, slowly, painstakingly, he maneuvered and strategized and planned—on the basis of an early trauma he witnessed coaching his college baseball team—and brought about the greatest change in the history of our national pastime. *It can be done.* Go to Cooperstown this summer and see the story unfold. It is well worth the three-hour drive. There is a sermon on the mound, not just on the mount but on the mound, preached in life, brought to voice through one lone Methodist, in one lone lifetime, in one lone sport, in one lone generation. Things can change for the better. *It can be done.* But you need a preacher, like Rickey: "I prefer the errors of enthusiasm to the reticence of wisdom."[11] *I prefer the errors of enthusiasm to the reticence of wisdom.*

Where is the Branch Rickey of American political culture? Where is the Branch Rickey of honesty about January 6, of preparation for the next pandemic, of the continuing struggle with racism, of the challenge of climate? Where is the Branch Rickey of Wall Street? Where is the Branch Rickey to waken the church, including his own beloved Methodism and mine? Where is the Branch Rickey of the urban public schools? Where is the Branch Rickey of your neighborhood? Where is that secular saint who doesn't realize it can't be done? Where is the preacher of the next sermon on the mound? And where are the actual preachers of the next generation who will remember and hope, as he did, in grace and freedom?

Maybe one is listening today. Maybe you are she. Things can change for the better, when sleepers awake.

---

11. Rickey, "Quotes."

Twenty years ago I heard William "Bobby" McClain, of blessed memory, a dear friend, a preacher of the first water from this school and this city, an African American pastor, tell about growing up in Tuskegee, Alabama. He grew up listening by radio to the team Branch Rickey fielded in Brooklyn. He said, "When Jackie stood at the plate, we stood with him. When he struck out, we did too. When he hit the ball, we jumped and cheered. When he slid home, we dusted off our own pants. When he stole a base, he stole for us. When he hit a home run, we were the victors. And when he was spiked we felt it, a long way away, down south. He gave us hope. He gave us hope."[12]

Don't let people tell you things can't change for the better. They can. This country can work. We just need a few more Branch Rickeys.

And a few more sermons on the mound . . . *And a few more sermons on the mound.*

So, dear friends, travel then with a little imagination . . . Imagine Eucharist at Marsh Chapel. Stand to sing . . . pause to reflect . . . step out into the aisle . . . look at and look past Abraham Lincoln and Francis Willard . . . receive cup and bread, bread and cup . . . kneel at the altar to pray . . . stand in communion with the communion of saints . . . Here is the bread and cup of friendship . . . Imagine a congregation reciting together a creed, a psalm, a hymn, a poem. Imagine, if you are willing, a congregation currently in diaspora, but just now, by the word spoken and heard, a gathered and thus addressable community, you and I and all together, able to prepare for the challenges, the harvests of the future, able to imagine and preach and live a kind of sermon on the mound.

---

12. From the author's memory, during a sermon at UMC North Central New York Annual Conference, 1995.

17

Faith Before Daybreak

Mark 1:4–11
Delivered at Boston University Marsh Chapel
January 10, 2021

A voice came from the heavens, "You are my Son, the Beloved; with you I am well pleased."[1]

THERE ARE SOME WEEKS when good news seems hard to come by.

Late in November 1963—with youth hockey around the corner, and, at last, some new skates that fit—a lingering pallor covered our town. President Kennedy had been tragically shot. There was an evening prayer service, but good news was hard to come by. "We are a nation drenched in sorrow," began Jan's dad's,[2] my father-in-law's, rewritten sermon for that Sunday.

---

1. Mark 1:11, NRSVUE.
2. Rev. Dr. Robert E. Pennock (1927-2019).

A decade later, with some of us studying abroad, preparing to teach college-level Spanish literature—a dream deferred to another lifetime—the war in Vietnam was reportedly ending, with helicopters carrying out the remaining soldiers and staff from a rooftop in Saigon. "How do you ask a man to be the last man to die for a mistake?"[3] aptly asked one then young, now veteran, national leader. A nation chastened, broken, without bearing or mooring, and little good news to be had.

A bit more than a decade later, in 1988, a plane down in Lockerbie—but we rehearsed that last week, did we not?

Of a Tuesday morning, a bright one, a bright autumn morning, September 2001, some of us headed out for work wondering what we had just seen—what had we seen?—in the skies above the Towers above the city that never sleeps. Little sleep and very little good news there was during that week of 9/11. The evenings were given over to community worship, and on Friday the churches, come eleven o'clock, were packed. The dangling chads of Broward County the year before were forgotten.

On this very avenue, in April of 2013, with the blasts of Beacon Street still reverberating in mind and memory, every evening that week brought, right in here in Marsh Chapel, some manner of worship service and gathering for healing and help. None of it fully adequate, all of it offered to God and neighbor on behalf of a better future day, days and weeks when there would be more news of a better sort. A promissory note within the notes of grief and loss.

Early November 2016 brought another set of days, a week, weeks, let us say, of confusion and despair regarding that fall's election. In hindsight, we see a bit better why. What many meant by "choices" in 2016 was not the meaning of those choices. What one meant was not, and is not, what it means. What you meant is not what it means. What it means is found not in intention but in consequence. The road to hell is paved with good intentions. We all can attest to that from our own experience and our own behavior. It was hard to scare up much good news that late autumn.

There are some weeks when good news seems hard to come by, and this week is one such. Yet these serial reminders of dark days past are meant, as you rightly surmise, to recall that we did make it through them, and we will get through this, too. *We did make it through them, and we will get through this, too.* Not unscathed, and hopefully not unchanged, but together, we will make it through.

3. Kerry, "Vietnam Veterans Against the War."

Already, coming into this week, we faced challenges aplenty. A climate reeling out of control. A pandemic claiming three hundred fifty thousand lives. A political culture—a culture-cooked politics, for politics is ever downstream from culture—putting people at daggers drawn. A community of communities seeing, in full, for the first full time, it may be, the ravages and damages of racial bias, hatred, and prejudice. And pain, the pain of every day.

Now this week. On top of all other, this (Thursday) morning's blaring headline, *Trump incites mob*.[4] Four dead, not in Ohio this time, but in the nation's capital city, and inside the nation's capitol building. Insurrection with presidential incitement. One wonders about the future of the party of Lincoln.

January 6, 2021. For the rest of history, for the rest of our lives, we shall have to live with, and attempt by faith to live down, both to live with and to live down, such utter calumny, such tragic, needless, heedless yet revelatory disaster. It is an apocalyptic—a revelatory—moment, hundreds wrecking the capitol, with hardly a single arrest to date, encouraged by a wantonly graceless leader, and with six senators, six senators (Cruz, Hawley, Hyde-Smith, Kennedy, Marshall, Tuberville) and much other congressional cattle[5] continuing to feed its root cause. For while this sermon is being recorded Thursday late afternoon, January 7, 2021, we cannot be at all sure what further difficulty and distress may visit us, during this current week of scarce good news, by Sunday, January 10, 2021, when the sermon is heard. I heard one say, "This is like 9/11, except we did this to ourselves."

But at some preconscious level, somewhere down in the declivities of the country's psyche, we had a sense that this was coming. We did not want to admit it. We hoped against hope to be wrong in that premonition. We hoped to whistle past the graveyard for another few days. Yet we remembered, dimly, from our upbringing: *Don't play with fire if you don't want to get burned.* We have had four years of warning, advisement, signs along the pathway of this premonition. So we are not surprised, and have no reason to be. It has been as plain as the nose on your face—even as plain as the nose on *my* face—at least since Charlottesville. It is no wonder, no surprise, that the Twenty-Fifth Amendment remedy is now rightly, and wisely, under full consideration. For a lot can happen in two weeks.

4. *Boston Globe*, "Trump-Incited Mob Attacks the Capitol," January 7, 2021.

5. A reference to Jonah 4:11, NRSVUE: "And should not I spare Nineveh, that great city, wherein are more than sixscore thousand persons that cannot discern between their right hand and their left hand; and also much cattle?"

So, the community of faith will gather, come Sunday, January 10, 2021, to listen, pray, and prepare. You have come this morning, by radio or internet, to listen, pray, and prepare. And to wonder. Just what is the gospel, the good news for this Lord's Day?

With you, I weep for my country and its people. More so, I pray for my own people, my own congregation, for our university, our listenership, for you and your loved ones, near or far or very far away. It must be admitted that there are some weeks when good news seems pretty hard to come by. This is one.

Still. The preacher's role is to announce the gospel in interpretation of and in accord with the Scriptures. Scripture gives us the chance for the long view. Scripture gives us a deep grounding, with heaven a little higher and earth a little wider. Thank goodness we have the Holy Scripture to which to turn, from which to learn, with which to listen, pray and prepare. "Silver and gold I have none, but such as I have give I thee."[6] Listen. Pray. Prepare.

Listen. The Gospel of Mark was written for listening. It emerged over a long time, with the earliest Christians reciting and recalling their Lord, his love, and their shared shaping by that love in faith, beginning in baptism. They listened, morning and evening, Sunday by Sunday, and over time, in direct response to weeks both empty and full, they began to write down for future generations what they had heard. Today we have such an account, that of Jesus's baptized. Today we have such a lesson, the hearing of a voice. Today we start again into an unknown future, within earshot of that same divine voice saying, *This is my beloved.* For all our failure, for all manner of sin and death and meaninglessness, for all that is wrong—and there is much, especially just now—there is a voice, ringing out and calling to us. A voice from heaven. "A voice came from the heavens, 'You are my Son, the Beloved; with you I am well pleased.'"[7] Yes, this is a scandalous particularity, to name one "the Beloved," to call out one with intimacy ("with you"), to identify one baptized in the Jordan: "With you I am well pleased." Yet for generations women and men have found this particularity strikingly universal and lastingly, eternally real. Especially in weeks when good news is scarce. And in our time, into dimensions of common ground that may cause us work and make us uncertain, we will want to learn to listen, and listen again. Listen. Listen. Listen.

---

6. Acts 3:6, KJV.
7. Mark 1:11, NRSVUE.

Pray. What a tremendous spiritual gift is our Psalter. Here are 700 years of psalms, 1000 to 400 BCE. Remember Samuel Terrien teaching us:

> For the psalmists, Yahweh's presence was not only made manifest in Zion. It reached men and women over the entire earth. . . . the sense of Yahweh's presence survived the annihilation of the temple and the fall of the state 587 B.C. Elusive but real, it feared no geographical uprooting and no historical disruption.
> . . . Having faced the void in history and in their personal lives, they knew the absence of God even within the temple . . . The inwardness of their spirituality, bred by the temple, rendered the temple superfluous.[8]

In other words, they knew how to live through and out through godless weeks. Our psalm today, Psalm 29, ancient and redolent with glory, recalls for us how to pray. From your youth, you have known. Adoration, confession, thanksgiving, supplication: the ACTS forms of prayer. Adoration, confession, thanksgiving, supplication. One is a word of glory, echoing the glory of God that thunders. *Glorify God and enjoy him forever.* A word of glory. One is a word of contrition, by which we begin every service at Marsh Chapel. Prayer is not only a matter of individual or even personal attention, a certain sitting silent before God. Prayer is also the voice, the responsive voice, of the people of God, echoing in antiphonal chorus, the call, the bowing before glory. *Glory!* All have sinned, all have fallen short of that primordial glory. All. A prayer of contrition. One is a word of gratitude. In such a week, it may simply be a prayer of gratitude that things are not yet any worse. A piercing memory from an eighty-seven-year-old person who had hidden, and been hidden, from the Nazis as a child evoked this the other day:

> During the war, we didn't know if we would make a day. I didn't have any freedom. I couldn't speak loudly, I couldn't laugh, I couldn't cry.
> But now, I can feel freedom. I stay by the window and look out. The first thing I do in the morning is look out and see the world. I am alive. I have food, I go out, I go for walks, I do some shopping. And I remember: No one wants to kill me. So, still, I read. I cook a little bit. I shop a little bit. I learned the computer. I do puzzles.[9]

A word of gratitude. One is a word of longing, desire, incantation, supplication. *Dear God, guide us through these murky moments, like those we have seen in the past, let us pray, and let our learning now make us stronger later.*

---

8. Terrien, *Elusive Presence*, 279.
9. Levy, "My Last Years," January 4, 2021.

A word of supplication. Prayer takes some set aside time, some quiet, some intentional focus. Pray. Pray. Pray.

Prepare. The whole of Scripture begins with the divine preparation, in creation and in speech. "Let there be . . ."[10] And what might that be, "let there be"? *Light.* Watch for the rays of light in the dark. *Watch for the rays of light in the dark.* Wednesday morning—before all, well, chaos, broke loose—a newly elected senator from Georgia was interviewed. He was raised in public housing, one of twelve children. Whatever the day, his dad had them all up before dawn. "Weeping may tarry for the night, but joy comes with the morning,"[11] he was reminded. *Yes, it's morning,* he responded, *but it's still dark.*[12] Senator Warnock learned to prepare, tying his shoes every morning, before daylight, to get ready, to be ready. His parents gave him the gift of faith before daybreak. So. *Light.* Watch for the coming rays of light. Nor does light shine only in the heart, but also, even more so, in the heart of the community. Individuals need to prepare, but so do communities. Senator Warnock went to Morehouse College, and was greeted by his dean: Founding Dean of the Martin Luther King Jr. Chapel, Rev. Dr. Lawrence Carter Sr., who has preached from this Marsh pulpit three times in the last three years. Now, Senator Warnock went on to earn a PhD from Union Theological Seminary in the City of New York (I believe I have heard of the school) and has since been in the pulpit of historic Ebenezer Church, Atlanta, for many years. But Dean Carter reminded me in conversation Wednesday morning that when Raphael Warnock's parents dropped him off at Morehouse, he had not a dime to his name. His parents could give him only what they had: their powerful, limitless, ceaseless love, pride, and belief in him. *Their powerful, limitless, ceaseless love, pride and belief in him.* Not much? Well. It seems to have been enough, just enough. That's the thing about the morning. It begins in the dark, in preparation, awaiting the word . . . *Let there be light.* Prepare. Prepare. Prepare.

People of God. Listen! Pray! Prepare! And hear, again, the Gospel:

"A voice came from the heavens, "You are my Son, the Beloved; with you I am well pleased."[13]

---

10. "Then God said, "Let there be light," and there was light." Gen 1:3, NRSVUE.
11. Ps 30:5, RSV.
12. Warnock, "Dawn," February 22, 2021.
13. Mark 1:11, NRSVUE.

18

Luminous Eye

Luke 9:28–36
Delivered at Boston University Marsh Chapel
February 27, 2022

Call to Confession

[Read earlier than the sermon, prior to the "Kyrie Eleison"]

EVEN AS WE GATHER in safety this morning, in a secure college community, we bear in mind other young women and men, like those now in Ukraine, who defend their homes, land, and families at great and sometimes ultimate cost. They bear the hard hurt and cost of learning, virtue, and piety[1]: learning, to distinguish truth from falsehood; virtue, to distinguish good from evil; piety, to distinguish life from death. We again face the bitter truth Dr. King named: "Injustice anywhere is a threat to justice everywhere."[2] For many of us, our thought, feeling, and thought-feeling—we dare say, our confession—is that there is more we can and should have done. May we be confessionally mindful, at least, of all those near and far, young and old,

---

1. "Learning, Virtue, Piety" is Boston University's motto.
2. King Jr., *I Have a Dream*, 85.

known and unknown, who face falsehood, evil, and death, and all those as well who yet lack shelter, raiment, safety, and nourishment.

Indeed, and in full, our minds and hearts dwell this day on the children, women, and men immersed in the tragic warfare that has been brutally and needlessly unleashed in and on Ukraine. We pray for them and for President Biden and other world leaders working to restore peace and justice. In particular, we hold close to our hearts those Boston University students and staff with homes and families in these regions. Our chaplains and staff are readily available for prayer, counsel, and support. Utterly realistic about the tragedy and harm now unfolding, we yet hold onto a distant hope for a better day to come, one day. As the choir sings the "Kyrie," may we again squarely face our dire, utter need for confession, awaiting a distant hope of pardon.

Luke

Today is Transfiguration Sunday. On the mountain, the baffled disciples tried to bear true witness—word, tent, accolade, mystery. What did you see? I saw . . .

Our passage from Luke 9 is an account developed after Easter as a way of trying to symbolize Jesus Christ as risen Lord. It has no biographical or earthly valence, nor does it need any, nor does it claim any. It is about seeing, and being transfigured by what one sees. The disciples see, truly saw, Jesus. "During Jesus' lifetime a few intimate followers were permitted a glimpse of what he was to become."[3]

Our witness arrives after a word and before a deed. Transfiguration precedes healing for the shrieking, convulsing, foaming-at-the-mouth demoniac, a case that stumped all disciples.[4] Transfiguration follows the word of the cross: "If any wish to come after me, let them deny themselves and take up their cross daily and follow me."[5]

A moment of witness follows a word and forecasts a deed.

You are good and sturdy gospel listeners, so you know, without elaboration, that Moses embodies the law and Elijah the prophets. You know the revelation of wisdom from Moses, the Decalogue.[6] Recite it by memory. You

---

3. Buttrick, ed., *Interpreter's Bible*, 8:173.
4. Luke 9:37-43, NRSVUE.
5. Luke 9:23, NRSVUE.
6. See: Exod 20:1-17, NRSVUE.

know the audition of love from Elijah. Remember the "still small voice."[7] (The Lord was not in the wind, earthquake, or fire . . . "and after the fire a sound of sheer silence."[8]) Sinai and Horeb, the Law and the Prophets.

Here, it is as if the Gospel of John has spilled ink upon the page of Saint Luke. Notice the little things: law and prophets, Moses and Elijah; a prophecy of the cross, called by the term "departure"[9] (did John write this?!?) (the Greek word is *exodos*); Andrew absent; Peter confused.

But what of his confusion? The confusion itself is confusing. "Not knowing what he said."[10] What does that mean? Jesus confuses Peter. Peter confuses Luke. Luke confuses the preacher of the day. The preacher confuses you. There is an opacity here, a stymied utterance. To which, oddly but honestly, Peter bears witness.

There is a cloud here, a cloud of unknowing. There is a mountain here, a mountain of unknowing. There is a voice here, a voice of unknowing. There is a countenance here, a face of unknowing. There is a white robe here, a robe of unknowing. There is a silence here. This is worship. Enchantment. Not entertainment. Enchantment, not entertainment. Bear witness.

Pandemic Gift

Poetry may illumine theology. Theology can ascend to poetry.

Ours is a scientific, not a poetic, age. We follow the science, not the poem. Yet, as Jaspers once remarked, perhaps we need continuously to "seek out that which contradicts us."[11]

Our maladies are many. Planet overheating. Pandemic marching. Politics infuriating. Prejudice remaining. Pocketbook straining. Putin attacking.

And, through it all: systems straining. Inequality increasing. Culture languishing. Doubts multiplying. Faith receding. Our maladies are many.

---

7. 1 Kgs 19:12, KJV.

8. 1 Kgs 19:12, NRSVUE.

9. "Who appeared in glory and spoke of his departure, which he was to accomplish at Jerusalem." Luke 9:31, RSV.

10. "Just as they were leaving him, Peter said to Jesus, 'Master, it is good for us to be here; let us set up three tents: one for you, one for Moses, and one for Elijah,' not realizing what he was saying." Luke 9:33, NRSVUE.

11. Szalai, review, January 10, 2022.

Yet in and through the long history of the communities of faith there are—there remain—springs of living water, there remain pools of quiet calm, there remain underground currents of life and hope and love. We, for sure and first, need all that we can muster to provide physical wellness: vaccine, booster, testing, tracing, masking, distancing, all. We do. But physical wellness alone will not see us through, will not carry us through, will not bring us through. In tandem with physical wellness, for a future worthy of its name, we shall—also and more so, it may be—need spiritual gladness. Physical wellness then leans toward, reaches up for, finds a path toward spiritual gladness. Wellness alone will not save. Gladness, too—that which makes the heart sing and the mind dance, gladness, a luminous inner eye of spiritual gladness—we shall need, to cool climate, deter pandemic, heal politics, sustain systems, dampen inflation, encourage culture, doubt our doubts, and find faith. Worship brings spiritual gladness. What brings you spiritual gladness? What gladness does this coming week promise? Where will you find such? How will you know it when you see it? What brings you spiritual gladness?

Two years ago, a week into the pandemic (which we then thought might abate by Easter, you may recall, my oh my), a friend and member of the Marsh Chapel worshipping community gave me a book. This is Dr. Ute Possekel of Harvard, who teaches Syriac there. She meant it, I believe, as a symbol of light, a little bit of light, as we then entered COVID dark. (Who would have thought we would be still shadowed so, twenty-four months later, with more to come?) I am grateful for her faithfulness and her gift, her gift of faith and her faith in the goodness of gifts. Today's sermon is simply a reflection on this marvelous gem of a book, a homiletical book report, you might say.

Her gift is *The Luminous Eye: The Spiritual World Vision of Saint Ephrem the Syrian,* by Sebastian Brock.[12] Brock sums up Ephrem thus:

> Ephrem is a theologian who employs poetry as the principal vehicle of his theology. Because of the way in which the study of theology has grown up in the West we have all too often forgotten that poetry can prove to be an excellent medium for creative theological writing. . . . [As in:]
>
> "It is not at the clothing of the words
> that one should gaze,
> but at the power hidden in the words."

---

12. Cistercian, 1992.

... The Syriac poetic medium through which Ephrem works has the added advantage of being completely free from the somewhat deadening literary conventions of the Graeco-Latin rhetorical tradition of late antiquity, conventions that can often seem tiresome to the modern reader.[13]

Theopoetic Life

Some will remember Kathleen Norris's memoir of thirty years ago, *Dakota: A Spiritual Geography*.[14] She intentionally centered her work on the seemingly contrary terms, spiritual and geography, stayed centered on that mash-up, and brought many, a generation ago, to a renewed sense of faith, of depth, of meaning, of grace, and of love—all delivered with more than a pinch of humor. Ephrem does something of the same, throughout a whole lifetime of prayer, study, and writing. Because he wrote in Syriac and focused on poetry, he is not well-known, especially compared to his fourth-century contemporaries (Basil, the Gregories, Athanasius).[15] He died in AD 373, was raised in a Christian home, and lived on today's Turkish-Syrian border in the Roman outpost of Nisibis, before moving late in life to Edessa. He spent much of his life and ministry in organizing relief for the poor, and led some sort of consecrated life short of full monasticism. (As you already perceive, there are many similarities here to the lives of John and Charles Wesley.) Ephrem was heir to three major traditions: ancient Mesopotamian tradition, Jewish tradition, and Greek tradition. Hence, he is an ideal meeting point between East and West.[16] *Do we not need more such today, even in this very hour?* With Athanasius, he battled the Arian "heresy" throughout his lifetime. In the course of his work and writing, both in poetry and prose, several magnificent insights arise as guides for our own lives.

13. Brock, *Luminous Eye*, 160–61.
14. Houghton Mifflin, 1993.
15. Brock, *Luminous Eye*, 13. "The Gregories" refers to Saint Gregory of Nazianzus and Saint Gregory of Nyssa.
16. Brock, *Luminous Eye*, 21.

Insights

One of Ephrem's primary insights is the steady reliance on the primacy of faith: "I believe in order that I may understand."[17] A second involves his celebration of human free will ("The nature of our free will is the same in everyone"[18]). A third, strikingly modern abiding insight is the "value of the body." In fact, Ephrem repeatedly uses imagery of clothing in his poetry. This may be related to his abiding dual reliance on Scripture and nature both: "God's two witnesses."[19] But all of this pales in comparison to the rhythmic beauty of his theopoetics:

> Your fountain, Lord, is hidden
> from the person who does not thirst for You;
> Your treasury seems empty
> to the person who rejects You.
> Love is the treasurer
> of your heavenly treasure store.[20]

> Truth and love are wings that cannot be separated,
> For Truth without Love is unable to fly,
> so too Love without Truth is unable to soar up:
> Their yoke is one of harmony.[21]

Most strikingly, Ephrem takes his poetic eye into the rendering of meaning in Holy Scripture. Scripture opens itself to the "eye of faith," and is open to multiple meanings. "God depicted His word with many beauties, so that each of those who learn from it can examine that aspect of it which he likes."[22]

> So brethren, let prying dry up and let us multiply prayers,
> for though He is not related to us, He is as though of our race,
> and though He is utterly separate, yet He is over all and in all.[23]

At the heart of Ephrem's teaching there lies a beautiful borderland, like the border areas in Tillich's existentialist theology. Listen to the poetic spirit:

---

17. Quoted in Schaff, *History of the Christian Church*, 5:602.
18. Quoted in Brock, *Luminous Eye*, 35.
19. Brock, *Luminous Eye*, 41.
20. Quoted in Brock, *Luminous Eye*, 44.
21. Quoted in Brock, *Luminous Eye*, 45.
22. Quoted in Brock, *Luminous Eye*, 50.
23. Quoted in Brock, *Luminous Eye*, 65.

> Lord, You bent down and put on humanity's types
> so that humanity might grow through Your
> self-abasement.[24]

We find also that "a sense of wonder gives rise to faith":[25]

> Blessed is the person who has acquired a luminous eye
> with which he will see how much the angels stand in awe of You, Lord,
> and how audacious is man.[26]

So for Ephrem, life becomes a pattern of listening, obedience, and faith. Give ear to his magnificent poetry, so utterly fit for Transfiguration Sunday:

Luminous Eye

> Illumine with Your teaching
> The voice of the speaker
> And the ear of the hearer:
> Like the pupil of the eye
> Let the ears be illumined,
> For the voice provides the rays of light.
>
> Praise to You, O Light.
>
> It is through the eye
> That the body, with its members,
> Is light in its different parts,
> Is fair in all its conduct,
> Is adorned in all its senses,
> Is glorious in its various limbs.
>
> Praise to You, O Light.
>
> It is clear that Mary
> Is the "land" that receives the Source of light;
> Through her it has illumined
> The whole world, with its inhabitants,
> Which had grown dark through Eve,
> The source of all evils.

24. Quoted in Brock, *Luminous Eye*, 54.
25. Quoted in Brock, *Luminous Eye*, 69.
26. Quoted in Brock, *Luminous Eye*, 73.

Praise to You, O Light.

Mary and Eve in their symbols
Resemble a body, one of whose eyes
Is blind and darkened,
While the other is clear and bright,
Providing light for the whole.

Praise to You, O Light.

The world, you see, has
Two eyes fixed in it:
Eve was its left eye,
Blind,
While the right eye,
Bright, is Mary.

Praise to You, O Light.

Through the eye that was darkened,
The whole world has darkened
And people groped
And thought that every stone
They stumbled upon was a god,
Calling falsehood truth.

Praise to You, O Light.

But when it was illumined by the other eye,
And the heavenly Light
That resided in its midst,
Humanity became reconciled once again,
Realizing that what they had stumbled on
Was destroying their very life.

Praise to You, O Light.[27]

---

27. Quoted in Brock, *Luminous Eye*, 71-73.

Mirror

Our poet theologian of the fourth century has carefully preceded us, cutting a trail forward in our reading of Scripture. For him, Scripture is a mirror, an ancient mirror, a distant mirror, but the crucial mirror; "This mirror is a figure of the holy preaching of the outward Gospel. . . . There the kingdom of heaven is depicted, visible to those who have a luminous eye."[28] The reading of Scripture, including its public recitation in worship at Marsh Chapel, for instance, is meant to further a "spiritual awareness, a reciprocation, no less, of divine love."[29] The reading of Scripture furthers "each individual's openness to the sense of wonder, and his or her possession of the luminous inner eye of faith."[30]

Ephrem celebrates the medicine of life, the coal of fire, the pearl of great price, the incarnation, the bridal chamber of the heart, the church as bride, all leading toward what this preacher would call a "modified" ascetic ideal: "The ideal of wakefulness, characteristic both of the angels and of the wise virgins, together with that of singleness, would thus seem to be among the most important motivating factors that lay behind the ascetic vision and orientation of early Syriac Christianity."[31] We have in our time the term "woke," but that sense of wakefulness was early and fully expressed *already* in the fourth century.

Sebastian Brock, our guide to and through the work of Saint Ephrem, challenges us with theological poetry today. He is the Rick Steves of the land of Ephrem. Ephrem represents a genuinely Asian form of Christianity, a great gift especially for those of us largely shaped by, saturated by, the European traditions. Ephrem "employs poetry as the *principal* vehicle of his theology."[32] While not inclined to eschew the historical, scientific, ethical, and moral demands of Scripture, Ephrem nonetheless steadily avers that the interpretation of Scripture comes within the context of faith. Further, in a most contemporary way, Ephrem's ecological vision, and his emphasis on the role of the feminine in faith, are for us added gifts in our time. We are not the first to honor the earth or to celebrate the strength of woman in faith and life. "Coming from the time of the undivided Church, Ephrem

---

28. Quoted in Brock, *Luminous Eye*, 77.
29. Brock, *Luminous Eye*, 84.
30. Brock, *Luminous Eye*, 96.
31. Brock, *Luminous Eye*, 141.
32. Brock, *Luminous Eye,* 160. (Italics mine.)

belongs to the heritage of all Christian traditions. He speaks to the unlearned and learned alike, to both lay and religious . . . precisely because his thought and imagery are so deeply rooted in the Bible, his poetry is thereby enabled to participate in something of the perennial freshness of the biblical text itself."[33] *The perennial freshness of the biblical text itself.*

May that perennial freshness kindle in us a spiritual gladness, this and every Lord's Day!

---

33. Brock, *Luminous Eye*, 172-73.

19

After Ten Years

John 20:19–31
Delivered at Boston University Marsh Chapel
April 16, 2023

Our shared faith provides a particular kind of memory, a powerful kind of prayer, and a persistent kind of love as hallmarks of Easter morning. Do they mark your life? Do memory, prayer, and love clothe life for you?

The gospel is resurrection in memory, in prayer, and in love. What empty space, what unoccupied tomb, abides in your life for these three, and for the greatest of these—love?

We set forth to do the work of facing grief with grace, failure with faith, hurt with hope, and death with dignity. And thee? Is that work begun, continued, or completed? The Word brings you life, brings you uplift, a lift for living, even "into the teeth of death,"[1] so you may face, face down, and live down death.

---

1. Whittier, "Palatine," st. 16.

Death makes us mortal. Facing death makes us human. The last enemy destroyed is death. We all, finally, shuffle off this mortal coil[2] . . . "God is doing in the world what it takes to make and to keep human life human."[3]

Seek "the Living One," he who is more alive than all life, whose life is the marrow of being alive. Why do you seek the Living One? *Ton zonta*[4]—a title perhaps, a person for sure, an announcement of Christ crucified and risen. All appearances to the contrary notwithstanding.

"The marks of the new age are at present hidden *in* the old age. . . . at the juncture of the ages the marks of the resurrection are hidden and revealed in the cross of the disciple's daily death, and *only* there."[5] We are to understand that this "is what the turn of the ages means: life is manifested in death."[6]

We need not overpreach. We still "walk by faith, not by sight."[7] We still "see in a mirror, dimly."[8] We still "have this treasure in earthen vessels."[9] We still "hope for what we do not see."[10] The resurrection follows but does not replace the cross.

"Paul gives no indication that he was familiar with the doctrine of the empty tomb. There is not the remotest reference to it in any of his letters, and his own conviction that the resurrection body is not the body of this flesh but a spiritual body waiting for the soul of man in heaven . . . makes it improbable that he would have found it congenial."[11]

Grace comes with the morning, every morning. So walk with the women—walk with me, too; let us walk together through the Gospel in sermon. And if you get done with the sermon before the sermon gets done—if you are finished with it before I am—have no fear, do not worry. Just wait a bit, and I will catch up with you! Some of you will arise inspired, and some of you will awake refreshed, and both outcomes are worthy outcomes!

---

2. A reference to Shakespeare, *Hamlet*, Act III, Sc. i., line 67.
3. Lehmann, *Ethics in a Christian Context*, 112.
4. From Greek: "living one," or "the living."
5. Martyn, "Epistemology," 110. (Italics in the original.)
6. Martyn, "Epistemology," 93.
7. 2 Cor 5:7, NRSVUE.
8. 1 Cor 13:12, RSV.
9. 2 Cor 4:7, KJV.
10. Rom 8:25, NRSVUE.
11. Buttrick, ed., *Interpreter's Bible*, 8:416.

We do not know what a day will bring. True this is of every day, but truer of some days than others. Focus, for a moment, on the gravest of days you have known. Someday I would like to hear of it.

Patriots' Day 2013 was such a day, ten years ago. We in this neighborhood learned firsthand about the visitation of death, tragically known again this week in Brussels and around the globe. Spelled $D \ldots E \ldots A \ldots T \ldots H$. Not your imaginary friend, but an equally omnipresent invisible enemy.

That Monday began with brunch and celebration and ended with terror, and needless slaughter, and (humanly speaking) unforgivable horror. Our staff opened the chapel later for the throngs walking, T-less,[12] by. Water, refreshment, prayer, counsel, they gave. One runner came very cold and was shrouded with a clergy gown, all we had to offer, a shepherd's outfit. What a week. Tuesday brought us to the plaza, come evening, in vigil, to honor and reflect. Wednesday, in this chapel, and also at other hours in other settings, gathered us for ordered worship, prayer, music, liturgy, Eucharist, and sermon. Thursday we heard President Obama on a familiar theme: running "the race set before us."[13] Friday we watched televised news at home. Saturday we listened for the musical succor of Handel's beautiful Messiah, right here. The Monday next we gathered again, for a memorial service for our deceased BU student, Lu Lingzi.

Death makes us mortal. Facing death makes us human.

You remember death. Your neighbor. Your hourly companion. You spell his or her name $D \ldots E \ldots A \ldots T \ldots H$. Easter morning is about intimations of life, the Living One outlasting death. Paul: "For as all die in Adam, so all will be made alive in Christ."[14] Behold: a glimmer of light in the dark, a rumor of life in death, an angel reclining in the tomb.

Memory gives us life.

If there has ever been an age that more needed better memory than ours, I know not what it would have been. "Those who cannot remember the past are condemned to repeat it."[15] "The past is never dead. It's not even past."[16] (Faulkner, whom I have been rereading this year.)

---

12. In Boston, the "T" refers to the public transit system, specifically the subway and aboveground trolleys.

13. "Let us run with perseverance the race that is set before us." Heb 12:1, NRSVUE.

14. 1 Cor 15:22, NRSVUE.

15. Santayana, *Life of Reason*, 1:284.

16. Faulkner, *Requiem for a Nun*, 85.

During that week journalists from around the globe contacted us and others across the university. Many, perhaps most, called or wrote from Asia. Some needed commentary for radio news or other newscasts. The main newspapers across the country also sent reporters.

On Wednesday, the chapel office took a call from *The Philadelphia Inquirer*. Could someone meet their man and his photographer at the steps of the chapel, to help convey something of the nightly vigils, services, and prayers of the week? We picked a mid-afternoon hour. In the April sunlight the interview began. Suddenly the photographer lowered his camera and shouted. *Bob! Bob! Bob!* His name is Clem Murray, a high school classmate and friend. He and his girlfriend Mimi Sinopoli were the "class couple" because they were the most beautiful couple, a truly stunning twosome. I had seen neither for forty years, from 1972 to 2013. I had heard that they married during college. Somehow, Clem recognized enough of my former self, hidden behind the current condition of my condition, and recognized my name. He let go of the camera for a hug. We finished the interview and photo. I turned then, as they were going, to ask, "So, how is Mimi?" You only know the really awkward moments too late. They come up after you, like alligators out of the Florida swamp. Clem said nothing. He didn't need to. I could see what he was holding back in his face and eyes. He just shook his head and shook. "Two years ago she died of cancer." In the midst of life we are in death, every moment. All I could see of her was a white graduation gown, a little cap and tassel. Three decades of marriage, three children, all things bright and beautiful, and then a malignancy unto death. Clem waved goodbye. A *kairos*, not a *chronos* moment . . .

We held, together, a memory of life that made life, that gave life, that made alive. In the very presence of death. It was a resurrection memory. A living memory takes you out of the present and into a living past. It was a resurrection memory. And perhaps the most powerful personal conversation I have known.

Marcel Proust, with his madeleine moment, teaches us best: "A single minute released from the chronological order of time has re-created in us the human being similarly released . . . situated outside the scope of time, what could one fear from the future?"[17] These are "resurrections of the past."[18]

Memory gives us life.

Prayer gives us life.

17. Proust, *Remembrance of Things Past*, 2:996.
18. Proust, *Remembrance of Things Past*, 2:1111.

A week after the Marathon, you may remember, we memorialized our student, Lu Lingzi. This service was held, as had been the memorial for President John Silber the autumn before, in the George Sherman Union. Twelve hundred attended, with an unknown number around the globe watching and listening by cybercast. The service proceeded, word and music, after careful attention and planning by musicians and clergy. We heard the Gospel of Mark and the Analects of Confucius. We listened to instrumental and choral music. We grieved, remembered, accepted, and affirmed, together. The family, eighteen or so and dressed in black, sat in the front row. As the service ended, from the next row, I could see and hear a susurration along the family pew. They then were meant to move to the gathering and greeting room, but no one stood. Further conversation moved up and down the row, in a language I could not understand. I feared: Have we forgotten a eulogy, or left out a reading, or skipped over an anthem? No. It was something else. After a moment, the family, dressed in black, stood as one, moved as one, turned as one, and faced the congregation and the world. A long quiet ensued. Then, as one, they bowed at the waist, and held the bow. To honor the gathering, to honor the moment, to honor the life, to honor Life, they bowed, in silence. It is the most powerful liturgical moment I have ever known. It was a resurrection prayer. And it is perhaps the most powerful liturgical moment I have seen.

"Different are the languages of prayer, but the tears are all the same."[19] We should repeat this three times a day.

Prayer gives us life. Prayer is a mode of existential gratitude.

Love gives us life.

The next Sunday, April 28, turned out to be a nice, warm early spring day. As the sun came up, we looked forward to a day of rest and worship, a chance for a return to normal.

About one hour before the Sunday service, our chaplain came in to the office to say, "We have another one." It took me some moment to understand and internalize the fact of another death. She had died tragically in a fire, caught in an upper room. Her mother would be coming up from New York City on the bus later that evening. The police would have informed her of her daughter's death. Our dean of students, Kenn Elmore, and his associate and I planned to meet the bus. That evening, while awaiting a delayed Greyhound, we talked a bit about the week past. We pondered how best to greet the grieving mom. It was decided I would meet the bus and

---

19. Heschel, *Insecurity of Freedom*, 180.

greet her as she came down the steps, to offer our heartfelt condolences and start the trek over to the hotel. The noise of the terminal, the lateness of the hour, the long weeks of terror and loss, and the approximate presence of death itself settled on us and gave us that quiet of the soul that sometimes overtakes us.

In the bus rolled. The mother came down the steps carrying a beautifully decorated box, holding it with both hands.

"I want to greet you for the University, and express our deepest sympathy and heartfelt concern," I said.

She replied, "Where is my daughter? What hospital is she in? Please take me to her, so I can see her and talk with her. I want to go and see her. Where is she? How is she doing? I brought a rice cake. See? In the box. It is her favorite rice cake. I know it will make her feel better."

At every phrase, I tried to say with honesty and kindness that her daughter had in fact died the night before, caught in an awful fire. Apparently she did not understand the police, or they did not speak clearly, or someone else in the family took the call. I tried everything. But she could not understand, or could not hear, until at last she looked up with intensity and asked, "You mean . . . she . . . is dead?" Yes.

There is a phrase in the Christmas Gospel about Rachel weeping for her children.[20] That bus terminal echoed with the chilling, haunting, painful cries of a mother who rightly could not and would not be consoled, as Rachel could not. The reverberation of her sobbing across that urban nighttime cacophony I can hear still. Nothing I said helped. Nothing I did helped. Nothing I could offer her could she receive. We sat on a bench, the wailing stronger still, the cake and box on the floor, the gathered friends lost in grief. Then she stiffened, her arm in mine becoming taut and cold. Perhaps she was going into shock. Everything I tried—counsel, prayer, listening, Scripture, all—was of no avail.

Then from her other side Dean Elmore simply surrounded, enfolded her. He put all of his body and arms all around her as she wailed and stiffened. He held her. He rocked her. He embraced her. And little by little, sob by sob, she began to slacken. And little by little, breath by breath, she began to loosen up. And little by little, held tight, she came through it. Her lament lessened, her limbs loosened. Out up from the tomb she came. A

---

20. "Then what had been spoken through the prophet Jeremiah was fulfilled: 'A voice was heard in Ramah, wailing and loud lamentation, Rachel weeping for her children; she refused to be consoled, because they are no more.'" Matt 2:17-18, NRSVUE.

physical, unspoken compassion brought her through from death to life. It was a resurrection love, compassion, embrace, grace, freedom, care, acceptance, mercy, pardon, peace, inclusion. It was a resurrection love. And it is perhaps the most powerful very public, pastoral ministry I have witnessed.

Unamuno: "Warmth, warmth, more warmth! for we die of cold, and not of darkness. It is not the night that kills, but the frost."[21]

Some years ago, at the time of our dad's death, Elie Wiesel sent a note. It was love physical, compassionate, and personal, and, as with all resurrection love, it made a difference. It concluded: "In our tradition we say: may you be spared further sorrow."[22]

Love gives us life.

Memory. Prayer. Love.

"The marks of the new age are at present hidden *in* the old age."[23] And "that is what the turn of the ages means: life is manifested in death."[24]

Easter, this season, is memory, prayer, and love; creation, redemption, sanctification; Father, Son, Spirit; life in death. And life in death holds out a promise of something grander still: life after death.

---

21. Unamuno, *Tragic Sense of Life*, 327.
22. Wiesel, personal correspondence with author, June 2010.
23. Martyn, "Epistemology," 110. (Italics in the original.)
24. Martyn, "Epistemology," 93.

20

Baccalaureate 2023

Address Delivered at Boston University
May 21, 2023

Graduates of the class of 2023:

As we gather, we celebrate your success; we honor our esteemed, excellent University leadership; we welcome your parents and friends; and we pause, briefly, with you, to ponder the meaning of it all.

(Usually, I have the responsibility to speak to the Baccalaureate guest, and, among other things, to gently but clearly remind them that they have just fifteen minutes for the Baccalaureate Address. Now the shoe is on the other foot, and I feel their pain: only fifteen minutes. The wheels of justice grind slow but exceedingly fine!)

So let me ask you to consider, *briefly,* three aspects of this high, holy moment, your graduation—all three of which are embedded in this Marsh Chapel, and embedded in the meaning of your study here.

Learning. Virtue. Piety.

Lifelong learning. Social virtue. Transformational piety.

We have, at Boston University, a strange, superstitious tradition regarding the seal embedded in front of Marsh Chapel, which by legend is not to be stood upon prior to completion of courses on the pain, threat, or supposition that one such misstep will block one's progress toward graduation itself, or at least somehow delay the degree.

For a few minutes at this Baccalaureate 2023, let me upend my own, and perhaps your own, puzzlement—even disregard—for this tradition. Just for a moment. For, like a lot of strange traditions, this one about not stepping on the seal may, oddly, have a point. For the seal has upon it three exacting words: words to live by, not just for a bit of life, but for the whole of life. Potent words. Words with electricity, juice, in them. Words, three words, not to be treated lightly, tread upon, scuffed, sauntered over, mistreated, marked or mocked with disdain. Words, three words fit to carry for the memory of Commencement, the beginning of the road away from school. Words, three words with which to make not just a living, but also to make a life. You and I do not believe in ghosts. Yet . . . we have our own reasons, over time, to accord some measure of respect—respectful agnosticism, but respect nonetheless—to the uncanny, to the numinous, to the strange, to the elusive, even when such are produced for us out of an odd legend. For life is haunted by things we don't see, things we don't understand, things we cannot control. Scripture and tradition acknowledge this—from the Midas touch to Lot's wife.

Here are three divine words, lasting truths, immutable markers of what matters, lasts, and counts. In the vigor of youth, and in the tempestuous vitality of young life, somehow, it may be our students are on to something. They are teaching us, and themselves. They are chary of, wary of, disdain for the true, the good, and the beautiful, in places of the heart, of the soul, of the subconscious. In good Shaker tradition, the heart follows the hand, their heart follows their feet. Put your hands to work, and your hearts to God. In three words.

The first of these is "learning." That means lifelong learning. As you entered the chapel, above the portal, there is the sculpture of Mr. John Wesley, whose Methodist movement gave BU birth in 1839, and who sang, "Unite the pair, so long disjoined, / Knowledge and vital piety: / Learning and holiness combined, / Truth and love [for all to see]."[1] *A kind of early "One BU."* He was devoted to learning, lifelong learning, as have been many of our guests here, over these years. In 2018, John Lewis (of blessed memory), Anthony Fauci, Carmen Yulín Cruz Soto (mayor of San Juan) all reminded us of this, both in speech and in example. They embodied the civil rights movement, the challenges in Puerto Rico (remember the

---

1. Wesley, "Prayer for Children," st. 5. (Bracketed words reflect changes from gender-based language found in the original.)

former president's graceless remarks about Puerto Rico that year?), and the importance of science in health (though we could not yet see the pandemic coming, nor Dr. Fauci's central leadership through it). Experience is the greatest teacher, especially when it causes us to learn through disappointment, but also when it causes us to learn through generosity.

Disappointment teaches us lessons that success cannot fathom. Faith mainly comes from trouble. Mr. Wesley and his early band of Methodists learned to "watch over one another in love"[2] because life is so shot through with disappointment. Wesley was two hundred years after Shakespeare, but he would have known the aching hurts recorded in those monumental plays and poems. You read Shakespeare at some point at BU, and so recall his 66th Sonnet, awash in disappointment:

> Tired with all these, for restful death I cry,
> As, to behold desert a beggar born,
> And needy nothing trimm'd in jollity,
> And purest faith unhappily forsworn,
> And gilded honour shamefully misplaced,
> And maiden virtue rudely strumpeted,
> And right perfection wrongfully disgraced,
> And strength by limping sway disabled,
> And art made tongue-tied by authority,
> And folly doctor-like controlling skill,
> And simple truth miscall'd simplicity,
> And captive good attending captain ill:
> Tired with all these, from these would I be gone,
> Save that, to die, I leave my love alone.[3]

We learn through experience, including the experience of grace—the grace, say, to overcome disappointment. That is faith, whether in secular or religious attire.

Likewise, we learn too through giving. You only have what you can give away, what you have the freedom and power to give away. You only truly possess what you have the liberty to give away.

So, two hundred years after Shakespeare, along came John Wesley, teaching a tithing generosity; Mr. John Wesley who greets us at the door, coming and going.

This morning we gather up in prayer the experiences of four years, and lift them all in a spirit of grace and peace.

2. Watson, "Methodists," 641.
3. Shakespeare, *Works*, 1039.

This morning we embrace the graduates of 2023 as they commence with the rest of life, and lift them all in a spirit of grace and peace.

This morning we open ourselves to the world around us and pledge ourselves to live not only *in* this world, but also—and more so—*for* this world, for this world in a spirit of grace and peace. Horace Mann: "Be ashamed to die until you have won some victory for humanity."[4]

John Wesley was the founder of Methodism, the religious tradition that in 1839 gave birth to Boston University. His motto: *Do all the good you can.*

The words are simple: that is significant.

The language is universal: that is significant.

The tone is thankful: that is significant.

The phrasing is memorable: that is significant.

These are words fit for use morning by morning, day by day, year by year, all in a lifetime. That, too, is significant.

> Do all the good you can,
> By all the means you can,
> In all the ways you can,
> In all the places you can,
> At all the times you can,
> To all the people you can,
> As long as ever you can.
> Do all the good you can.[5]

Learning, lifelong learning.

The second of the three words embedded in the central, haunted plaza seal, the occult and subconscious dark backdrop of life—life, as Hobbes said, that is "solitary, poor, nasty, brutish, and short"[6]—the second of these words is "virtue." That means social virtue. That means common, civic, communal virtue. Your class has known the importance of shared, national virtue, which was needed to overcome a raging pandemic that impacted every one of you—every one of us. Your class lived through the raging furies of January 6, 2021, which had the potential to impact every one of you—every one of us. Your class lived through the surges of isolation, anxiety, and depression that continue to challenge us.

---

4. Mann, "Baccalaureate Address of 1859," 1:575.

5. Sometimes called "John Wesley's Rule of Life," these lines are likely a paraphrase of passages from various of Wesley's sermons. See especially: Wesley, "Use of Money," 675.

6. Hobbes, *Leviathan*, 84.

Well, we have a second permanent guest in Marsh Chapel, a fellow who knew much about this. He is in the back corner on the pulpit side, up in stained glass. Lincoln, Abraham Lincoln. He is reminder that virtue is the bedrock of shared, national, social, cultural life. Real leaders have virtue. Virtue is not optional in a nation's leadership. Shun mendacity. We may differ about the size and scope of a budget, or the most apt programs in foreign affairs. But we cannot differ about telling the truth, about personal virtue, about lies, including big lies. Personal virtue, especially in leaders, is the basis for national virtue. Class of 2023, in warning, we say: Do not be fooled, here. On this, "a house divided against itself cannot stand."[7]

Remember who you are and whose you are. Listen to the few paragraphs of Lincoln's greatest words. Listen for the anaphora in the beginning, and the epistrophe at the end. Listen to the gravity and realism, but listen also—out of a dark corner and hour—for the hope.

> Fourscore and seven years ago our fathers brought forth upon this continent a new nation, conceived in liberty, and dedicated to the proposition that all men are created equal.
>
> Now we are engaged in a great civil war, testing whether that nation, or any nation so conceived and so dedicated, can long endure. We are met on a great battle-field of that war. We have come to dedicate a portion of that field as a final resting-place for those who here gave their lives that that nation might live. It is altogether fitting and proper that we should do this.
>
> But in a larger sense, we can not dedicate, we can not consecrate, we can not hallow this ground. The brave men, living and dead, who struggled here, have consecrated it far above our power to add or detract. The world will little note nor long remember what we say here, but it can never forget what they did here. It is for us, the living, rather, to be dedicated here to the unfinished work which they who fought here have thus far so nobly advanced. It is rather for us to be here dedicated to the great task remaining before us; that from these honored dead we take increased devotion to that cause for which they gave the last full measure of devotion; that we here highly resolve that these dead shall not have died in vain; that this nation, under God, shall have a new birth of freedom; and that government of the people, by the people, and for the people, shall not perish from the earth.[8]

---

7. Lincoln, *Speeches*, 95.
8. Lincoln, *Speeches*, 323–25.

Both history and mystery are at the heart of a regard for virtue, and at the heart of any real college education.

Virtue, social virtue.

The third of these three words is perhaps the strangest to our ears, but maybe the most important. It is "piety." That means transformational piety. This year Jonathan Eig has published *King: A Life*,[9] a biography of Martin Luther King. King lived to transform. Real piety is transformative. The piety here, the faith here, in your old BU bones, is transformational—not just personal, but transformational piety.

My dad was born in the same year as King, and was here as a student at the same time. My dad was raised by a single mom, with no dad at home. But not all of our parents are natural parents. Some are relational parents. He met a teacher, a homiletics teacher here at BU, who became such—a relational, not natural parent—and so, when their first child was born, he and his wife gave their child the middle name "Allan" after that teacher, Allan Knight Chalmers. That child is the rascal speaking to you now. None of us got here alone. Others helped; others practiced a transformational piety. Thank one, two, or three of them today, if you have a chance.

There is no greater voice, near or far, of transformational piety than that voice celebrated in the heart of our plaza. For your meditation, here are selected epigrams from your fellow BU alumnus, the Reverend Dr. Martin Luther King Jr.

"Only when it is dark enough, can you see the stars."[10]

"Say that I was a drum major for justice . . . for peace . . . for righteousness."[11]

"Darkness cannot drive out darkness; only light can do that. Hate cannot drive out hate; only love can do that."[12]

Faith is taking the first step even when you don't see the whole staircase.[13]

---

9. Farrar, Straus and Giroux, 2023.
10. King Jr., *I Have a Dream*, 195.
11. King Jr., *I Have a Dream*, 191.
12. King Jr., *Strength to Love*, 47.
13. Often attributed to King, this quote is likely a paraphrase of his words as heard by Marian Wright Edelman, who during several interviews ascribed similarly-worded statements to King. See: *And Still We Rise: Interviews With 50 Black Role Models*, ed. Barbara A. Reynolds (Washington, D.C.: USA Today, Gannett, 1988), 74-75; and Marian Wright Edelman, "Kids First!" *Mother Jones* 16, no. 31 (May-June 1991), 77.

"I believe that unarmed truth and unconditional love will have the final word."[14]

"The arc of the moral universe is long but it bends toward justice."[15]

"I have a dream my four little children will one day live in a nation where they will not be judged by the color of their skin but by the content of their character."[16]

"You gotta have a dream; if you don't have a dream, how you gonna have a dream come true?"[17] Have some dreams, even if, as Nina Tassler told us in 2016, you have to edit your dreams.[18] It would be great to have some of the children of King—Rafael Warnock, Deval Patrick, Marilynne Robinson, Barack Obama—here in autumn 2025 to celebrate the seventy-fifth anniversary of the dedication of Marsh Chapel. May we find the grace to seek and serve his cause of justice in the years to come.

A story, one of transformational piety, which King repeatedly told, is of Marian Anderson. She was awarded an honorary degree here at Boston University in 1960, a Black opera singer whose voice was perhaps the greatest of all in the last century. But it was her mother who made it possible:

> I remember when Marian was growing up, and I was working in a kitchen till my hands were all but parched, my eyebrows all but scalded. I was working there to make it possible for my daughter to get an education. . . .
>
> And finally one day somebody asked Marian Anderson in later years, "Miss Anderson, what has been the happiest moment of your life? Was it the moment that you had your debut in Carnegie Hall in New York?" She said, "No, that wasn't it." "Was it the moment you stood before the kings and queens of Europe?". . . "Was it the moment that Toscanini said that a voice like yours comes only once in a century?" "No, that wasn't it.". . . And she looked up and said quietly, "The happiest moment in my life was the moment that I could say, 'Mother, you can stop working now.'" Marian Anderson realized that she was where she was because somebody helped her to get there.[19]

---

14. King Jr., *I Have a Dream*, 110.
15. King Jr., *I Have a Dream*, 179.
16. King Jr., *I Have a Dream*, 104.
17. Rodgers and Hammerstein II, *South Pacific*.
18. "Don't be afraid to edit your dreams and rewrite the story of what you want to do in life." Tassler, "Commencement Address," May 15, 2016.
19. King Jr., *Knock at Midnight*, 153-54.

And somebody helped you, too.

Piety, transformative piety.

Learning. Virtue. Piety. Personal. National. Global. Lifelong. Social. Transformative. They are your words, now, now that you have crossed the seal; your words, chiseled in the stone of Marsh Chapel; your words, embodied in the beauty of this chapel with Wesley and Lincoln and King. Nod to Mr. Wesley, to President Lincoln, to Dr. King, in sculpture and window and monument, as you depart. But, Class of 2023: carry them in memory, not for a day but for a lifetime.

> Let love be genuine; hate what is evil; hold fast to what is good; love one another with mutual affection; outdo one another in showing honor. Do not lag in zeal; be ardent in spirit; serve the Lord. Rejoice in hope; be patient in affliction; persevere in prayer. Contribute to the needs of the saints; pursue hospitality to strangers.[20]

Class of 2023: bon voyage!

---

20. Rom 9-13, NRSVUE.

Bibliography

Adams, Abigail, and John Adams. *My Dearest Friend: Letters of Abigail and John Adams.* Edited by Margaret A. Hogan and C. James Taylor. Cambridge: Belknap, 2007.
Albright, W. F., and C. S. Mann, trans. *Matthew.* Vol. 26 of *The Anchor Bible.* Garden City, NY: Doubleday, 1971.
Allen, Woody, dir. *Annie Hall.* United States: United Artists, 1977.
Anderson, Wes, dir. *Moonrise Kingdom.* United States: Focus Features, 2012.
Andrews, Edward G., ed. *The Doctrines and Discipline of the Methodist Episcopal Church.* New York: Eaton & Mains, 1904.
Augustine. *Confessions of St. Augustine.* Translated and edited by Albert Cook Outler. Mineola, NY: Dover, 2002.
———. *On Christian Doctrine.* Translated by J. F. Shaw. In *On Christian Doctrine; The Enchiridion; On Chatechising; and On Faith and the Creed,* 1-171. Vol. 9 of *The Works of Aurelius Augustine, Bishop of Hippo,* edited by Marcus Dods. Edinburgh: T. & T. Clark, 1873.
———. *Soliloquies, Book I.* Translated by Charles C. Starbuck. In *St. Augustin: Homilies on the Gospel of John; Homilies on the First Epistle of John; Soliloquies,* 537-47. Vol. 7 of *A Select Library of the Nicene and Post-Nicene Fathers of the Christian Church,* edited by Philip Schaff. New York: Christian Literature, 1888.
Babcock, Maltbie D. "God," also known as "This is My Father's World." Translated by Frederic Henry Hedge. In *The Methodist Hymnal: Official Hymnal of the Methodist Church,* no. 72. New York: United Methodist Publishing, 1939.
Berger, Peter L. *A Rumor of Angels.* New York: Doubleday, 1969.
Bonhoeffer, Dietrich. *The Cost of Discipleship.* Translated by R. H. Fuller. Revision by Irmgard Booth. From the German *Nachfolge* (1937). New York: Simon & Schuster, 1959.
———. *Letters and Papers from Prison.* Edited by Eberhard Bethge. Enlarged ed. New York: Macmillan, 1972.
Bradbury, Ray. *Fahrenheit 451.* New York: Simon & Schuster, 1967.
Brock, Sebastian. *The Luminous Eye: The Spiritual World Vision of Saint Ephrem the Syrian.* Rev. ed. Kalamazoo: Cistercian, 1992. First published 1985 by C. I. I. S., Rome.

Brown, Robert McAfee. *Elie Wiesel: Messenger to All Humanity*. Notre Dame, IN: University of Notre Dame Press, 1989.
Buttrick, George Arthur, ed. *The Interpreter's Bible*. 12 vols. New York: Abingdon, 1951-52.
Calvin, John. *Commentary upon the Epistle of Saint Paul to the Romans*. Translated and edited by Henry Beveridge, from the original English translation by Christopher Rosdell. Edinburgh: Calvin Translation Society, 1844.
———. *Harmony of the Gospels: Matthew, Mark, and Luke*. Vol. 1 of *Calvin's Commentaries*, translated by A. W. Morrison, edited by David W. Torrance and Thomas F. Torrance. Grand Rapids: Wm. B. Eerdmans, 1972.
Camus, Albert. *The Rebel: An Essay on Man in Revolt* [*L'Homme révolté*]. Translated by Anthony Bower. New York: Vintage, 1956.
Coffin, William Sloane. *Collected Sermons: The Riverside Years*. Vol. 1. Louisville: Westminster John Knox, 2008.
———. *Credo*. Louisville: Westminster John Knox, 2006.
Craig, David J. "Thurman Center Director Shares Broad View of Race Relations," *B. U. Bridge* iv, no. 17 (December 15, 2000).
Darwin, Charles. *On the Origin of Species*. New York: D. Appleton, 1870.
Dickinson, Emily. "Experience." In *Poems*, 3rd series, edited by Mabel Loomis Todd, 68. Boston, MA: Roberts Bros., 1896.
———. *The Poems of Emily Dickinson: Reading Edition*. Edited by R. W. Franklin. Cambridge: Belknap, 1999. See esp. "Tell all the truth but tell it slant—" (1263).
Faulkner, William. *Go Down, Moses*. Reprint. New York: Random House, 1942.
———. *Requiem for a Nun*. London: Chatto & Windus, 1919.
Finley, James. *Merton's Palace of Nowhere*. Notre Dame, IN: Ave Maria, 1978.
Franklin, Benjamin. "Poor Richard's Almanac, 1735." In *Bartlett's Familiar Quotations*, edited by Justin Kaplan, 319. 17th ed. Boston: Little, Brown, 2002.
Gottwald, N. K. "Song of Songs." In *The New Interpreter's Dictionary of the Bible*, vol. 4, R-Z, 420-26. Reprint. Nashville: Abingdon, 1991.
Hammarskjöld, Dag. *Markings*. Translated by Leif Sjöberg and W. H. Auden. New York: Alfred A. Knopf, 1965.
Hartley, J. F. "My Life Flows On in Endless Song." In *The Lesser Hymnal: A Collection of Hymns, Selected Chiefly from the Standard Hymn-Book of the Methodist Episcopal Church*, no. 279. New York: Nelson & Phillips, 1875.
Hempton, David. *Methodism: Empire of the Spirit*. New Haven: Yale University Press, 2005.
Heschel, Abraham Joshua. *The Insecurity of Freedom*. Reprint. New York: Schocken, 1966.
———. *The Sabbath*. New York: Farrar, Straus & Young, 1951.
Hirschman, Albert O. *Exit, Voice, and Loyalty: Responses to Decline in Firms, Organizations, and States*. Cambridge, MA: Harvard University Press, 1970.
Hobbes, Thomas. *Leviathan: Or the Matter, Forme & Power of a Commonwealth, Ecclesiasticall and Civill*. Edited by A. R. Waller. Cambridge: University Press, 1904.
Hugo, Victor. *The Letters of Victor Hugo*. Edited by Paul Meurice. Boston: Houghton Mifflin, 1898.
Irenaeus. "Selections from the Work Against Heresies by Irenaeus, Bishop of Lyons: 'The Refutation and Overthrow of the Knowledge Falsely So Called.'" In *The Library of Christian Classics*, edited by John Baillie, John T. McNeill, and Henry P. Van Dusen. Vol. 1, *Early Christian Fathers*, translated and edited by Cyril Richardson, 358-97. Philadelphia: Westminster, 1953.

BIBLIOGRAPHY

John of the Cross, Saint. "Noche oscura del alma" ["The Dark Night of the Soul"]. Translated by David Lewis. London: Thomas Baker, 1908.

Johnson, James Weldon. "The Creation." In *God's Trombones: Seven Negro Sermons in Verse*, 17–20. New York: Viking, 1927.

Kerry, John F. "Vietnam Veterans Against the War, Speech Before the U.S. Senate Committee on Foreign Relations." In *Legislative Proposals Relating to the War in Southeast Asia, United States Senate Committee on Foreign Relations*, 92th Congress (1971). https://voicesofdemocracy.umd.edu/kerry-speech-before-the-senate-committee-textual-authentication/.

Kierkegaard, Søren [Johannes Climacus, pseud.]. *Philosophical Fragments*. Translated and edited by David F. Swenson and Howard V. Hong. Introduction and commentary by Niels Thulstrup. 2nd ed. Princeton, NJ: Princeton University Press, 1962.

King Jr., Martin Luther. *I Have a Dream: Writings and Speeches that Changed the World*. San Francisco: HarperSanFrancisco, 1992.

———. *A Knock at Midnight: Inspiration From the Great Sermons of Reverend Martin Luther King, Jr*. Edited by Clayborne Carson and Peter Holloran. New York: Warner, 1998.

———. *Strength to Love*. Gift ed. Minneapolis: Fortress, 2010.

———. *A Testament of Hope: The Essential Writings and Speeches of Martin Luther King, Jr*. Edited by James Melvin Washington. San Francisco: Harper, 1991.

Lazarus, Emma. "The New Colossus," lines 10–14. November 2, 1883. https://www.nps.gov/stli/learn/historyculture/colossus.htm.

Lehmann, Paul. *Ethics in a Christian Context*. London: SCM, 1963.

Leslie, Elmer. *The Psalms: Translated and Interpreted in the Light of Hebrew Life and Worship*. New York: Abingdon-Cokesbury, 1949.

Levy, Toby. "Covid-19 is Taking My Last Years." *New York Times*. January 4, 2021.

Lewis, John. Interview by Washington University in St. Louis and Blackside, Inc. November 6, 1985. http://repository.wustl.edu/concern/videos/x346d590n.

Lincoln, Abraham. *Abraham Lincoln's Speeches*. Edited by L. E. Chittenden. New York: Dodd, Mead, 1896. See especially: "Remarks at the Dedication of the National Cemetery at Gettysburg, November 19, 1863," 323–25, and "The Second Inaugural Address," 358–61.

Littell, Franklin. *The Crucifixion of the Jews*. New York: Harper & Row, 1975.

Lowell, James Russell. "The Present Crisis." In *Poems of James Russell Lowell*, edited by Nathan Haskell Dole, 199–203. New York: Thomas Y. Crowell, 1898.

Luther, Martin. "Majesty and Power," also known as "A Mighty Fortress is Our God." Translated by Frederic Henry Hedge. In *The Methodist Hymnal: Official Hymnal of the Methodist Church*, no. 67. New York: United Methodist Publishing, 1939.

Mann, Horace. "Baccalaureate Address of 1859." In *Life of Horace Mann*, by Mary Mann, 2nd ed. Vol. 1 of *Life and Works of Horace Mann*, 554–75. Boston: Walker, Fuller, 1865.

Marcus, Joel. *Mark. A New Translation with Introduction and Commentary*. Vol. 27 of *The Anchor Bible*. New York: Doubleday, 2000–2009.

Marquard, Bryan. "Rev. Wells Grogan; shared his struggle with church." *Boston Globe*, January 20, 2011. ProQuest Recent Newspapers.

Martyn, J. Louis. "Epistemology at the Turn of the Ages." In *Theological Issues in the Letters of Paul*, 89–110. Nashville: Abingdon, 1997.

———. *Galatians: A New Translation with Introduction and Commentary.* Vol. 33A of *The Anchor Bible*, edited by William Foxwell Albright and David Noel Freedman. New York: Doubleday, 1997.

Miller, Julie. "'A republic if you can keep it': Elizabeth Willing Powel, Benjamin Franklin, and the James McHenry Journal." *Unfolding History* (blog). Library of Congress, January 6, 2022. https://blogs.loc.gov/manuscripts/2022/01/a-republic-if-you-can-keep-it-elizabeth-willing-powel-benjamin-franklin-and-the-james-mchenry-journal/.

Moltmann, Jürgen. *Theology of Hope: On the Ground and the Implications of a Christian Eschatology.* Minneapolis: Fortress, 1993.

Pierson, Delavan Leonard. *Arthur T. Pierson: A Spiritual Warrior.* Self-published, 2012. eBook PDF. https://www.wholesomewords.org/biography/biorppierson.html.

Proust, Marcel. *Remembrance of Things Past.* Vol. 2. New York: Random House, 1949.

Redford, Robert, dir. *A River Runs Through It.* United States: Columbia Pictures, 1992.

Rickey, Branch. "Branch Rickey Quotes." Azquotes.com. https://www.azquotes.com/author/12336-Branch_Rickey.

Rodgers, Richard, and Oscar Hammerstein II. *South Pacific.* United States: Williamson Music (ASCAP), 1949. https://rodgersandhammerstein.com/song/south-pacific/happy-talk/

Royce, Josiah. "The Office of the Reason." In *The Bross Lectures, 1911,* 80–116. New York: Charles Scribner's Sons, 1912.

Santayana, George. *The Life of Reason: Or the Phases of Human Progress.* Vol. 1, *Introduction & Reason In Commonsense.* 2nd ed. London: Charles Scribner's Sons, 1905.

Schaff, Philip. *History of the Christian Church.* Vol. 5. Grand Rapids: Wm. B. Eerdmans, 1991.

Schweitzer, Albert. *The Quest of the Historical Jesus: A Critical Study of Its Progress from Reimarus to Wrede.* Translated by W. Montgomery. 2nd English ed. London: Adam & Charles Black, 1911.

Shakespeare, William. *The Works of William Shakespeare.* Edited by William George Clark and William Aldis Wright. Globe ed. Cambridge: Macmillan, 1864.

Smith, Samuel Francis. "My Country, 'Tis of Thee," 1831.

Szalai, Jennifer. Review of *Aftermath: Life in the Fallout of the Third Reich, 1945–1955,* by Harald Jähner. *New York Times,* January 10, 2022. ProQuest Recent Newspapers. https://www.proquest.com/pdnnewyorktimes/docview/2622638989/B1096CB53C474C91PQ/3?accountid=9676&sourcetype=Newspapers.

Tassler, Nina. "Commencement Address to Boston University's Class of 2016." Boston University, Boston, MA, May 15, 2016.

Terrien, Samuel. *The Elusive Presence: Toward a New Biblical Theology.* San Francisco: Harper & Row, 1978.

The Methodist Church. *The Book of Worship for Church and Home.* Nashville: Methodist Publishing House, 1945.

Thoreau, Henry David. *The Writings of Henry David Thoreau.* Vol. 1, *A Week on the Concord and Merrimack Rivers.* Reprint. Boston: Houghton Mifflin, 1906.

Tillich, Paul. *Systematic Theology.* Vol. 3, *Life and the Spirit; History and the Kingdom of God.* Chicago: University of Chicago Press, 1963.

Thurman, Howard. *Jesus and the Disinherited.* New York: Abingdon-Cokesbury, 1949.

———. *The Search for Common Ground: An Inquiry Into the Basis of Man's Experience of Community.* New York: Harper & Row, 1971.

Unamuno, Miguel de. "El sepulcro de don Quijote" ["The Sepulcher of Don Quixote"]. In *Vida de Don Quixote y Sancho*, 3rd ed., 2–27. Madrid: Renacimiento, 1928. English translation in *Essays and Soliloquies*, translated by J. E. Crawford Flitch, 82–98. New York: Alfred A. Knopf, 1925.

———. *The Tragic Sense of Life in Men and in Peoples*. Translated by J. E. Crawford Flitch. London: Macmillan, 1921.

Warnock, Raphael G. "Dawn." Facebook, campaign video by MoveOn, February 22, 2021. https://www.facebook.com/share/v/1NHMVioVDF/.

Watson, Richard. "Methodists." In *A Biblical and Theological Dictionary*, 640–45. Vol. 2. Rev. ed. New York: T. Mason & G. Lane, 1837.

Wesley, Charles. "Love Divine, All Loves Excelling." In *The Methodist Hymnal: Official Hymnal of the Methodist Church*, no. 372. New York: United Methodist Publishing, 1939.

———. "A Prayer for Children." In *Wesley's Hymns and the Methodist Sunday-School Hymn-Book*, no. 473. London: Wesleyan Methodist Sunday-School Union, 1886.

Wesley, John. "The Use of Money." In *Sermons on Several Occasions*, 662–75. New ed. Leeds: Edward Baines, 1744.

———. *The Works of the Rev. John Wesley, A.M.* Vol. 12, 3rd ed. corrected. London: John Mason, 1830.

West, Cornel. *Hope on a Tightrope*. United States: SmileyBooks, 2008.

Whitman, Walt. *Leaves of Grass*. Inclusive ed. Garden City, NY: Doubleday, Page, 1925.

Whittier, John Greenleaf. "The Palatine." In *Atlantic Monthly*, January 1867, 51–53. https://www.theatlantic.com/magazine/archive/1867/01/the-palatine/628712/.

Wiesel, Elie. *Night*. Translated by Stella Rodway. New York: Hill & Wang, 1960.

Wilder, Thornton. *Our Town: A Play in Three Acts*. New York: Harper & Row, 1957.

Winthrop, John. "A Model of Christian Charity." In *Bartlett's Familiar Quotations*, edited by Justin Kaplan, 246. 17th ed. Boston: Little, Brown, 2002.

Yeats, William Butler. "The Second Coming." In *Michael Robartes and the Dancer*, 19–20. Churchtown: Cuala, 1920.

www.ingramcontent.com/pod-product-compliance
Lightning Source LLC
Chambersburg PA
CBHW071431160426
43195CB00013B/1868